New Daylight

Edited by **Sally Welch**   September–December 2019

- 7 **Beacon words of promise**
  Elizabeth Rundle — *1–14 September*

- 22 **Success and failure**
  Veronica Zundel — *15–28 September*

- 37 **Francis and Clare**
  Helen Julian CSF — *29 September–12 October*

- 52 **1 Kings 17—22: The importance of being earnest**
  Fiona Stratta — *13–26 October*

- 67 **Exile (Part 2)**
  Andy John — *27 October–9 November*

- 82 **Psalm 119**
  Stephen Rand — *10–23 November*

- 97 **Glory**
  Geoff Lowson — *24 November–7 December*

- 112 **Making the most of Advent: 'The God who comes'**
  David Winter — *8–21 December*

- 127 **Christmas in Matthew**
  Sally Welch — *22–31 December*

The Bible Reading Fellowship
15 The Chambers, Vineyard
Abingdon OX14 3FE
brf.org.uk

The Bible Reading Fellowship (BRF) is a Registered Charity (233280)

ISBN 978 0 85746 779 9
All rights reserved

This edition © The Bible Reading Fellowship 2019
Cover image and illustration on page 141 and image on page 145 © Thinkstock

Distributed in Australia by:
MediaCom Education Inc, PO Box 610, Unley, SA 5061
Tel: 1 800 811 311 | admin@mediacom.org.au

Distributed in New Zealand by:
Scripture Union Wholesale, PO Box 760, Wellington
Tel: 04 385 0421 | suwholesale@clear.net.nz

Acknowledgements
Scripture quotations marked with the following acronyms are taken from the version shown. Where no acronym is given, the quotation is taken from the same version as the headline reference. **NRSV**: The New Revised Standard Version of the Bible, Anglicised Edition, copyright © 1989, 1995 by the Division of Christian Education of the National Council of the Churches of Christ in the USA. Used by permission. All rights reserved. **NIV**: The Holy Bible, New International Version, Anglicised edition, copyright © 1979, 1984, 2011 by Biblica. Used by permission of Hodder & Stoughton Publishers, an Hachette UK company. All rights reserved. 'NIV' is a registered trademark of Biblica. UK trademark number 1448790. **GW**: GOD'S WORD, © 1995 God's Word to the Nations. Used by permission of Baker Publishing Group. **Phillips**: The New Testament in Modern English by J.B. Phillips copyright © 1960, 1972 J.B. Phillips. Administered by The Archbishops' Council of the Church of England. Used by Permission. **NLT**: The Holy Bible, New Living Translation, copyright © 1996, 2004, 2015 by Tyndale House Foundation. Used by permission of Tyndale House Publishers, Inc., Carol Stream, Illinois 60188. All rights reserved. **CEV**: Contemporary English Version Copyright © 1991, 1992, 1995 by American Bible Society, Used by Permission. **CJB**: Complete Jewish Bible by David H. Stern. Copyright © 1998. All rights reserved. Used by permission of Messianic Jewish Publishers, 6120 Day Long Lane, Clarksville, MD 21029. messianicjewish.net. **TPT**: The Passion Translation. Copyright © 2017, 2018 by Passion & Fire Ministries, Inc. Used by permission. All rights reserved. ThePassionTranslation.com. **MSG**: The Message, copyright © 1993, 1994, 1995, 1996, 2000, 2001, 2002 by Eugene H. Peterson. Used by permission of NavPress. All rights reserved. Represented by Tyndale House Publishers, Inc. **GNT**: Good News Translation in Today's English Version – Second Edition Copyright © 1992 by American Bible Society. Used by permission. **NKJV**: New King James Version. Copyright © 1982 by Thomas Nelson. Used by permission. All rights reserved. **NEB**: The New English Bible (New Testament) © 1961 The Delegates of the Oxford University Press and the Syndics of the Cambridge University Press. **BCP**: *The Book of Common Prayer*, the rights in which are vested in the Crown, is reproduced by permission of the Crown's Patentee, Cambridge University Press. **ESV**: The Holy Bible, English Standard Version, copyright © 2001 by Crossway, a publishing ministry of Good News Publishers. Used by permission. All rights reserved.

A catalogue record for this book is available from the British Library

Printed by Gutenberg Press, Tarxien, Malta

Suggestions for using New Daylight

Find a regular time and place, if possible, where you can read and pray undisturbed. Before you begin, take time to be still and perhaps use the BRF Prayer on page 6. Then read the Bible passage slowly (try reading it aloud if you find it over-familiar), followed by the comment. You can also use *New Daylight* for group study and discussion, if you prefer.

The prayer or point for reflection can be a starting point for your own meditation and prayer. Many people like to keep a journal to record their thoughts about a Bible passage and items for prayer. In *New Daylight* we also note the Sundays and some special festivals from the church calendar, to keep in step with the Christian year.

New Daylight and the Bible

New Daylight contributors use a range of Bible versions, and you will find a list of the versions used opposite. You are welcome to use your own preferred version alongside the passage printed in the notes. This can be particularly helpful if the Bible text has been abridged.

New Daylight affirms that the whole of the Bible is God's revelation to us, and we should read, reflect on and learn from every part of both Old and New Testaments. Usually the printed comment presents a straightforward 'thought for the day', but sometimes it may also raise questions rather than simply providing answers, as we wrestle with some of the more difficult passages of scripture.

New Daylight is also available in a deluxe edition (larger format). Visit your local Christian bookshop or BRF's online shop **brfonline.org.uk**. To obtain a cassette version for the visually impaired, contact Torch Trust for the Blind, Torch House, Torch Way, Northampton Road, Market Harborough LE16 9HL; +44 (0)1858 438260; **info@torchtrust.org**. For a Braille edition, contact St John's Guild, Sovereign House, 12–14 Warwick Street, Coventry CV5 6ET; +44 (0)24 7671 4241; **info@stjohnsguild.org**.

Comment on *New Daylight*

To send feedback, please email **enquiries@brf.org.uk**, phone **+44 (0)1865 319700** or write to the address shown opposite.

Writers in this issue

Andy John is the Bishop of Bangor, where he has served for nine years. Andy is a Kiwi (his mother's side) and Welsh (his father's side) cross and has spent all his ministry in the Church in Wales. Apart from being a bishop, he occasionally attempts marathons (Snowdonia being a favourite) and enjoys time with his now grown-up children.

Helen Julian CSF is an Anglican Franciscan sister and a priest, currently serving her community as minister general. She has written three books for BRF and has contributed to BRF's *Quiet Spaces*.

Geoff Lowson is a retired priest living in a small village in the west of County Durham. In addition to parochial ministry, he spent 21 years working for the mission agency USPG.

Stephen Rand is a communicator who worked with Tearfund and Open Doors, travelling widely. He is now responsible for the public communications of the All-Party Parliamentary Group for International Freedom of Religion or Belief. He and his wife Susan live in Bicester, Oxfordshire, where Stephen is working on missional outreach to the new-build estates.

Elizabeth Rundle has written many study and devotional books including *Twenty Questions Jesus Asked* (BRF, 2008). She has written and presented scripts for local and national radio and television and organised and led 16 pilgrimages to the holy land. A retired Methodist minister, Elizabeth served churches in Cornwall and London.

Fiona Stratta is a speech and language therapist, speech and drama teacher, and the author of *Walking with Gospel Women* (BRF, 2012) and *Walking with Biblical Women of Courage* (BRF, 2017). Through her writing, she desires to connect readers' spiritual journeys more closely to their daily lives.

David Winter is retired from parish ministry. An honorary Canon of Christ Church, Oxford, he is well known as a writer and broadcaster. His most recent book for BRF is *Heaven's Morning* (2016).

Veronica Zundel is an Oxford graduate, writer and columnist. She lives with her husband and son in north London. Her most recent book is *Everything I Know about God I've Learned from Being a Parent* (BRF, 2013).

Sally Welch writes...

'There is a time for everything, and a season for every activity under the heavens' (Ecclesiastes 3:1, NIV).

These words never resonate more strongly with me than at the beginning of autumn, as the leaves turn golden, yellow and brown then drop to the floor, a morning chill becomes noticeable and the evening light fades ever more quickly. For some, autumn is a season of new beginnings – classes and societies begin again, there is a renewed energy apparent in the briskness of action after the languor of heated summers, new resolutions are made as familiar routines are picked up after the holidays. In keeping with this mood, Geoff Lowson tells us that the word 'glory' appears in the Bible 456 times and encourages us to wonder at the changing seasons, noticing that 'not only is creation showing forth God's glory, but creation itself is offering glory to God' and encouraging us to join in. Fiona Stratta's exploration of some of the stories in 1 Kings draws us into a greater appreciation of the wideness of God's mercy and the greatness of his plan for his children, calling us to celebrate his love for each one of us.

However, some of us are filled with gloom at the approach of winter, dreading the oncoming darkness and cold. Elizabeth Rundle begins our issue by showing us how the many promises God has given us shine out like beacons in our times of darkness, both physical and emotional, offering comfort and hope. Andy John in his exploration of 'exile' reminds us that the 'dark night of the soul' we might experience does not mean an absence of God, simply that we do not recognise his presence, and that often it is only after the time of 'exile' has ended that we appreciate all that we have learnt. Veronica Zundel, too, contributes to our understanding of difficult and challenging times by reminding us that often 'apparent success is really failure and apparent failure really success' and encouraging us to see these two concepts through God's eyes, not the world's.

Whatever your feelings about the coming season, I pray that the reflections in this issue will help you in your onward journey, that God will reveal himself to you in new ways and that your faith and understanding will grow and deepen.

Sally Ann Welch

The BRF Prayer

*Almighty God,
you have taught us that your word is a lamp for our feet
and a light for our path. Help us, and all who prayerfully
read your word, to deepen our fellowship with you
and with each other through your love.
And in so doing may we come to know you more fully,
love you more truly, and follow more faithfully
in the steps of your Son Jesus Christ, who lives and reigns
with you and the Holy Spirit, one God forevermore.
Amen*

Introduction

Beacon words of promise

A remark by one of my tutors at theological college left a deep and lasting impression on me. Turning pink with emphasis he declared, 'Don't ever start your prayers by saying, "Lord, we come into your presence." You are never *out* of his presence!' Few things from those faraway lectures have stuck in my mind so vividly, and over the next days I would like to share with you scriptural snippets which remind us that in whatever circumstance we may find ourselves, the God of Abraham, Isaac and Jacob, the God and Father of our Lord Jesus Christ, is ever present. I like to call these gems of encouragement 'beacon words of promise'.

Throughout the Bible, promises keep popping up for individuals as well as the nation at their point of need. In mystery and miracle, the 'voice' of God has been discerned by human hearts and minds, and over some 4,000 years, millions of believers have testified to this incomparable truth. It is both humbling and challenging to realise that hundreds of thousands of men and women who have been persecuted and murdered for their faith have taken comfort in these same promises. It is also troubling that, as you read these notes, somebody somewhere in the world will be in grave danger because of their faith.

Come with me and explore these 'beacon words of promise'. We begin way back in the time of aural history when stories of God's deliverance were shared around desert campfires, that universal method of passing down songs, stories and warnings, in the hope that listeners would take courage, learn compassion and seek justice. The apostle Paul wrote to young Timothy, 'All scripture is God-breathed and is useful for teaching, rebuking, correcting and training in righteousness' (2 Timothy 3:16, NIV). We'll move through the era of the great prophets and poets and find God's promises reiterated by Jesus. Finally, we read some verses in the book of Revelation and see how the promise of God's eternal presence becomes the torch of faith for generations past, present and future to follow. To quote the apostle Peter, 'The promise is for you and your children and for all who are far off – for all whom the Lord our God will call' (Acts 2:39, NIV). That includes us!

ELIZABETH RUNDLE

Sunday 1 September   **Genesis 28:14–16 (NIV, abridged)**

Wake-up call

'Your descendants will be like the dust of the earth, and you will spread out to the west and to the east, to the north and to the south. All peoples on earth will be blessed through you and your offspring. I am with you and will watch over you wherever you go…' When Jacob awoke from his sleep, he thought, 'Surely the Lord is in this place, and I was not aware of it.'

So many portions of scripture hold multilayered meaning. We shouldn't be surprised at this, because a snapshot of our own lives will doubtless be similarly multilayered. Jacob, grandson of Abraham and Sarah, and one of the most significant names in the Hebrew scriptures, is bluntly recorded warts and all.

To be honest, we all have character traits of which we are not proud, and it's tempting to hide behind a mask. God knows our weaknesses better than we do, yet his love does not discriminate but lifts us up to glimpse his presence. Masks may help us cope in the short term, but we must never let our masks hide what, with God's help, we can become.

Imagine Jesus listening to Jacob's story in the Nazareth synagogue. The first thing that leaps out at me is the way God will use a person regardless of their dubious backstory. A second truth is that for Jacob, exhausted physically, emotionally and spiritually, the last thing on his mind was God's presence. Maybe you have been in a similar desolate place. Grasp then the phenomenal core of this passage – *God was there*! Despite everything, God was with Jacob, promising to be with him always. When I am exhausted in mind and body, those four little words fill me with new courage: 'I am with you.'

I think about pictures on the news when there has been an earthquake and rescuers have found a survivor. Relief and even joy shine in the survivor's face – they are not alone; thank God, someone is with them. Is there someone you need to be with today?

Thank God for those who have been 'the hands of Christ' to you.

ELIZABETH RUNDLE

Monday 2 September Exodus 3:10–12; 4:13 (NRSV, abridged)

Unwilling servant

'So come, I will send you to Pharaoh to bring my people, the Israelites, out of Egypt.' But Moses said to God, 'Who am I that I should go to Pharaoh, and bring the Israelites out of Egypt?' He said, 'I will be with you... when you have brought the people out of Egypt, you shall worship God on this mountain'... But [Moses] said, 'O my Lord, please send someone else.'

Stories from the Bible were more familiar to me as a child than nursery rhymes. The lady who brought me up imparted her love of these ancient tales into my eager imagination, but it was not until mature adulthood that I realised Moses' reluctance to follow God's calling.

Not an overwhelmingly successful start for Moses! If we were choosing someone for such a monumental task, we too would be irritated by such a response. But before we condemn Moses for his lack of trust, remember he had murdered an Egyptian, so if he returned to Egypt his own life would be in danger. No wonder Moses was hesitant.

Have you ever had that sinking feeling when you have been asked to do something, but it is the very last thing you want to do? Or do you recall a heavy silence in a meeting when volunteers have been requested? Everybody longs for that certain 'someone else' – *anyone* else, Lord, but not me! A lesson I learnt early in my ministry was that tasks, sometimes unexpected and demanding tasks, were not entirely dependent on me. God provides us with helpers who have complementary gifts and graces, and to whatever situation we are called, we go not in our own strength but in the power of the Holy Spirit. Whatever task awaits you today, hold on to the promise, God is with you.

'If I ascend to heaven, you are there; if I make my bed in Sheol, you are there. If I take the wings of the morning and settle at the farthest limits of the sea, even there your hand shall lead me, and your right hand shall hold me fast' (Psalm 139:8–10).

ELIZABETH RUNDLE

Tuesday 3 September   **Joshua 1:7–9 (NRSV, abridged)**

Encouragement

'Only be strong and very courageous, being careful to act in accordance with all the law that my servant Moses commanded you; do not turn from it to the right hand or to the left... This book of the law shall not depart out of your mouth; you shall meditate on it day and night, so that you may be careful to act in accordance with all that is written in it... I hereby command you: Be strong and courageous; do not be frightened or dismayed, for the Lord your God is with you wherever you go.'

I've found this message to long-ago Joshua full of contemporary relevance and encouragement. It's not a 'don't be frightened, pull yourself together' type of encouragement; it's loaded with promise, God's divine promise that wherever, however or whatever we are, we are not alone. Almighty God is with us to hold, guide, direct and inspire.

God's command to Joshua to be strong and courageous came at the most crucial time of his life. Moses was dead. That towering personality who had faced up to Pharaoh and led the slaves out of Egypt, who had received the ten commandments on Mount Sinai, Moses his leader, teacher, adviser, parent and holy man was out of the picture – dead. How could Joshua possibly manage without him? I have known many times when key people have either moved or died and I have wondered what on earth would happen next. Joshua and I are not alone in our discovery that when a key person is no longer around, there will always be someone else to take on that role. Life carries on to new horizons and opportunities.

Joshua took courage from God's promise. Surely it is a miracle that some 3,500 years after Joshua we have the same book of the law in our Old Testament. Amazingly God's command and promise stand true today for you and me. Our Bible is not there just to look good on the shelf or beside the bed, but also to read and inwardly digest. We can be strong and courageous – our God is with us.

Hear the Lord Jesus say to you, 'Do not let your hearts be troubled, and do not let them be afraid' (John 14:27).

ELIZABETH RUNDLE

Wednesday 4 September — Psalm 46:1–3, 10–11 (NIV)

Calm down and listen

God is our refuge and strength, an ever-present help in trouble. Therefore we will not fear, though the earth give way and the mountains fall into the heart of the sea, though its waters roar and foam and the mountains quake with their surging… He says, 'Be still, and know that I am God; I will be exalted among the nations, I will be exalted in the earth.' The Lord Almighty is with us; the God of Jacob is our fortress.

What a superb mixture we have in the book of Psalms. If you want to rant and rave about the unfairness of life, if you want to worship and adore, if you want to look back and wonder at God's guidance or if you just want to sing praises, Psalms is your manual. Biblical scholars calculate that this psalm has been sung for over 28 centuries, which links us with our forebears in faith and, most significantly, with our Lord and Saviour, Jesus. The heading for this psalm defines it as 'a song', underlining the ancient pairing of music and worship.

The opening statement reminds me that God is not exclusive – not 'my' God. It is an inclusive statement, 'our' God. All over the world today, right this minute, people are longing for the peace of God's presence.

I find the words 'Be still' a challenge. I may not literally run through the daily chores and ever-lengthening 'to do' list, but it is still frustratingly difficult to take time out, to be still and vulnerable before God. These verses stand like a mini symphony, the bold opening notes before the pounding tumult of earthquake, fire and flood. Then the exquisite calm and beauty of stillness conclude with the climactic flourish, the promise that the Lord Almighty is with us. It's a psalm that leaves us on the high notes of confidence that whatever happens, even if our world disintegrates, God, our God, is with us. This is the spiritual reality of Immanuel, 'God with us'. I dare to ask myself, did Jesus love this psalm too?

Is there a piece of music that calms you? Maybe you have a favourite hymn. Be still, hum the tune and repeat the words. Know that God is with you.

ELIZABETH RUNDLE

A voice to your heart

Thus says God, the Lord, who created the heavens and stretched them out, who spread out the earth and what comes from it, who gives breath to the people upon it and spirit to those who walk in it: I am the Lord, I have called you in righteousness, I have taken you by the hand and kept you; I have given you as a covenant to the people, a light to the nations, to open the eyes that are blind, to bring out the prisoners from the dungeon, from the prison those who sit in darkness.

'It was the best of times, it was the worst of times.' So wrote Charles Dickens at the beginning of *A Tale of Two Cities* (1859). How apt for the plight of Isaiah's audience. The people felt God had deserted them, but into their mood of despair the prophet declares good news – God's people have a hope and a future. The 'voice' of God came to dispirited people with fresh, tender intimacy.

In times of uncertainty, in the face of defeat, depression and despair, God is never more close and personal. If we take a careful look at this beacon promise, we find that it is no saccharine platitude. It is what you could call a 'promise plus': God has never deserted his people and never will. I believe it is a promise as relevant in our world full of tragedy and uncertainty as it has been in every generation. This is where we touch the unique, layered quality of prophecy. At one level the proclamation is directly to a nation (it is tempting to see the promise of God's Messiah). But there is also another layer: God's promise to 'hold' and 'keep' us can be translated as to 'support' and 'cherish'. In being blessed with his presence, we can respond by being a blessing to others. Into the lives of those whose spiritual eyes have dimmed with grief, for those in the dungeon of despair or the prison of loneliness, let us pray for the light of Christ to penetrate their worst of times. Hold on to the promise that 'the light shines in the dark, and the dark has never extinguished it' (John 1:5, GW).

'Hear' the words of Jesus; 'Do not fear, for I am with you.'

ELIZABETH RUNDLE

Friday 6 September   **Isaiah 43:1–3a (NRSV, abridged)**

In life's storms

But now thus says the Lord, he who created you, O Jacob… Do not fear, for I have redeemed you; I have called you by name, you are mine. When you pass through the waters, I will be with you; and through the rivers they shall not overwhelm you; when you walk through the fire you shall not be burned, and the flame shall not consume you. For I am the Lord your God, the Holy One of Israel, your Saviour.

I lived for many years in Britain's most westerly county, with its 300 miles of coastline – beautiful Cornwall. In good weather the sea sparkles below majestic cliffs and beaches fill with sunseekers basking in full summer glory. Yet the seas are littered with the wrecks of old ships overwhelmed by thunderous, crashing waves. Inland, devastating floods have been recorded and tragic fires have taken life, ravaged moorland and ruined livelihoods. Such is the elemental and terrifying power of fire and water. I have been on a small boat tossed like a toy in unexpected heavy seas: parts were creaking and breaking; it seemed certain the boat would disintegrate at any minute and, yes, I was afraid!

It's hardly surprising we use terms related to nature to describe particularly difficult moments. We speak of the 'storms' of life and of situations creating 'dark clouds'; we 'sink' under a raft of expectations; we have 'floods' of tears; and many people 'burn' with anger. I am reminded of emotive words by the 19th-century American lawyer and hymn-writer H.G. Spafford: 'When sorrows like sea-billows roll, whatever my lot, Thou hast taught me to know, it is well with my soul.' Isaiah spoke God's promise to a distraught, fearful community, overwhelmed by events beyond their control. They all had the received memory of the ancient slaves leaving Egypt through the waters, but it was a great leap of faith to accept God's guidance in their day.

At this very moment, in too many countries, in too many homes and too many hearts, people are feeling overwhelmed by circumstance. People of every age need to hear these living words of promise today.

Lord, I pray for all who are crushed and afraid.

ELIZABETH RUNDLE

Saturday 7 September   Jeremiah 1:4–8 (NRSV)

God holds the future

Now the word of the Lord came to me saying, 'Before I formed you in the womb I knew you, and before you were born I consecrated you; I appointed you a prophet to the nations.' Then I said, 'Ah, Lord God! Truly I do not know how to speak, for I am only a boy.' But the Lord said to me, 'Do not say, "I am only a boy"; for you shall go to all to whom I send you, and you shall speak whatever I command you. Do not be afraid of them, for I am with you to deliver you, says the Lord.'

Taking a baby in my arms for baptism is always a powerful and emotional moment. What does the future hold for this tiny (or not so tiny) scrap of humanity? What difficulties will they encounter? What national, international or personal tragedies will challenge or change them? Will they be hurt by others or will they themselves be perpetrators of hurt? To them and every child before them, life is an exciting, precious gift, a blank canvas on which the colours of fear, anger, rejection, laughter, friendship and love will mould each character and personality.

As I think back on the young Jeremiah, I can imagine his parents' pride and their many expectations of their boy. As the son of a priest, Jeremiah would have enjoyed food, clothing and education beyond those of other boys in the village of Anathoth. He obviously showed a maturity and spirituality that marked him out. Nevertheless, from the record of how his life took shape over some 40 years of prophecy, we know Jeremiah faced rejection, persecution and suffering. I feel sure this man of God was sustained by the promise given to him in his youth – 'Do not be afraid, for I am with you.' We too can be confident that whatever happens, our God is with us – always.

O love of God, our shield and stay through all the perils of our way; eternal love, in thee we rest, for ever safe, for ever blest (Horatius Bonar, 1808–89).

ELIZABETH RUNDLE

Sunday 8 September   Jeremiah 31:31, 33–34 (NRSV, abridged)

A personal relationship

The days are surely coming, says the Lord, when I will make a new covenant… this is the covenant that I will make with the house of Israel… says the Lord: I will put my law within them, and I will write it on their hearts; and I will be their God, and they shall be my people. No longer shall they teach one another… 'Know the Lord', for they shall all know me, from the least of them to the greatest, says the Lord; for I will forgive their iniquity, and remember their sin no more.

One of the most overused words in advertising is 'new'. A new product implies it is improved: a new car will be more fuel-efficient and economical than the old; a new phone has the attraction of added apps and gismos. Oh, our human striving towards all things new! Here, in these words from the prophet Jeremiah, a man who had by this time endured beatings, ridicule and imprisonment, we are given an awe-inspiring vision: God will forgive the people, wipe the slate clean and move them from the old ways into a new, personal relationship. Old covenants had failed because they depended on people's faithfulness to God; the new covenant, however, was dependent on God's faithfulness to the people. God's faithfulness will never fail.

What a pity that when we think of the phrase 'the battle for hearts and minds', our thoughts fly to contemporary battlefields and areas of conflict. But God is also in a battle, a battle against sin in order to live in our hearts and minds. Legalism is cold and empty, we could say soul-less, but the new covenant invites us to respond to love. Whatever battles you are fighting, however thick the clouds of gloom, God's promise is a shaft of divine light. No other religion offers such personal connection: 'God so loved the world that he gave his only Son, so that everyone who believes in him may not perish but may have eternal life' (John 3:16).

Lord, in this new day, help me to nurture your law in my heart.

ELIZABETH RUNDLE

Monday 9 September   Matthew 28:16–20 (NRSV)

A promise for life!

Now the eleven disciples went to Galilee, to the mountain to which Jesus had directed them. When they saw him, they worshipped him; but some doubted. And Jesus came and said to them, 'All authority in heaven and on earth has been given to me. Go therefore and make disciples of all nations, baptising them in the name of the Father and of the Son and of the Holy Spirit, and teaching them to obey everything that I have commanded you. And remember, I am with you always, to the end of the age.'

We can never underestimate the power of language and it is amazing the impact one phrase can make. Five small words that Jesus spoke in his resurrection appearance offer us the means to transform our day and even our lives. Some time ago, talking with a group of children, I suggested they hold up their right hand and, touching each finger in turn, speak aloud the five words 'I am with you always'. I told them that whenever they felt anxious they could repeat Jesus' promise and know he was with them. I also suggested that they could respond to that promise by repeating the words on their left hand. It is an easy format to remember, as well as making the point that a relationship with the living Lord Jesus is not a one-way street. Jesus gives that promise to all believers, but it is up to each believer to accept and respond.

    Many Bibles add a heading to the end of Matthew's gospel: 'The great commission'. This is true, but there is a greater truth behind the words. Suddenly the phrase from the Old Testament that signified the name of God, 'I am' (Exodus 3:14), has transformed into Jesus himself: '*I am* with you always.' Meditate and soak up his words. Can you hear Jesus speaking across the centuries, across every culture and to any age group? Whatever you are doing today, Jesus speaks this promise directly to *you*. Receive Jesus' words of comfort and strength, transforming words to lift your spirit and give you hope.

Reflect on the words by Frances Jane van Alstyne (1820–1915): 'I am thine, O Lord; I have heard thy voice and it told thy love to me.' Thanks be to God!

ELIZABETH RUNDLE

Tuesday 10 September — John 14:1, 18–19, 27 (NRSV)

You are never alone

'Do not let your hearts be troubled. Believe in God, believe also in me… I will not leave you orphaned; I am coming to you. In a little while the world will no longer see me, but you will see me; because I live, you also will live… Peace I leave with you; my peace I give to you. I do not give to you as the world gives. Do not let your hearts be troubled, and do not let them be afraid.'

Were you an orphan? Have you become an orphan? Do you know anyone who is an orphan? There will certainly be orphans in your village, town or city.

It is shocking to read that there are an estimated 140 million orphans worldwide. As I write this page, the eyes of the world are focused on the plight of Syria and the Rohingya refugees in Bangladesh. Such trouble and fear are a devastating indictment on this century.

Men and women have confided in me the strange feeling that suddenly smothers them when both their parents have died. It is extra to the normal feelings of bereavement; they feel an emptiness, often a real fear and an unexpected isolation that compounds their grief. It may be in the natural rhythm of life to lose both parents eventually, but that does nothing to prepare you for or to negate the trauma of realisation. Interesting then that Jesus should highlight this emotive situation of being an orphan with the departure of his physical presence from his devoted followers.

These verses, most usually heard at funeral services, give me comfort. In the relationship we choose with Jesus, we will never be left on our own. His peace, his shalom, is the gift of a centred confidence that, in Christ, is the ultimate well-being. We may not understand, we may wrestle and get ourselves in a state, but the human face of God, our Lord Jesus Christ, will never leave us or forsake us.

A man came to Jesus and said, 'I believe; help my unbelief!' (Mark 9:24). Today, Lord, help me to still my anxieties. Give me your shalom, your peace in my heart.

ELIZABETH RUNDLE

Wednesday 11 September **Romans 8:35, 37–39 (NIV)**

Reassurance for Romans – and us!

Who shall separate us from the love of Christ? Shall trouble or hardship or persecution or famine or nakedness or danger or sword?… No, in all these things we are more than conquerors through him who loved us. For I am convinced that neither death nor life, neither angels nor demons, neither the present nor the future, nor any powers, neither height nor depth, nor anything else in all creation, will be able to separate us from the love of God that is in Christ Jesus our Lord.

What a statement of faith! Paul was writing to groups of early Christians gathered to worship in a city full of pagan gods. Rome, the hub of the empire, was crowded with people from every country around the Mediterranean, people Paul had never met. I find it fascinating to piece together links in the chain that first spread Christianity. In Acts, we read that 'visitors from Rome' were present on the day of Pentecost (Acts 2:10). Were those visitors the nucleus for the first congregations in Rome? Paul praises these new Christians for their faith 'reported all over the world' (Romans 1:8). How easy for us to focus on the great apostle Paul and overlook the courage and dynamism of those initial converts, both Jew and Gentile. God used Paul not just to express faith for first-century Romans, but also to give hope and inspiration down the centuries. This is the enduring miracle of living scripture.

Paul's catalogue of situations might seem to us somewhat dramatic, but, in only a few years, those same worshippers in Rome would themselves undergo the severest persecution. These verses assured them of God's everlasting love and presence. And while we may not feel particularly persecuted, there is a widespread fear of death, of evil forces and of what the future will hold. Whatever fears you may have today, read again this clarion cry from Paul: in essence, whatever happens, *nothing* on earth can separate us from God's unending love through Jesus.

'O Love that wilt not let me go, I rest my weary soul in thee'
(George Matheson, 1842–1906).

ELIZABETH RUNDLE

Thursday 12 September — Philippians 4:10–13 (Phillips, abridged)

The life within

It has been a great joy to me that after all this time you have shown such interest in my welfare. I don't mean that you had forgotten me… Nor do I mean that I have been in actual need, for I have learned to be content, whatever the circumstances may be. I know now how to live when things are difficult and I know how to live when things are prosperous… I am ready for anything through the strength of the one who lives within me.

I enjoy looking back at pictures from past holidays and events. Whether stored on the phone, on CDs or in old albums, they are lovely to recall. Sometimes, though, or more times than I care to admit, I have forgotten the incident or the person. I'm sure this was the case with the good folk at Philippi. Their days were filled with family, work and the million things that make up life, and although Paul had been a huge influence, when he was far away, he slipped out of their immediate focus.

We all do this, but the adage 'out of sight, out of mind' does not necessarily mean 'don't care'. Our brains just cannot hold everything up front, so a quiet time at the beginning or end of the day, or both, enables us to have a breathing space – moments to take stock, give thanks and regroup our priorities. Precious moments, steadying moments, healing moments.

These are moments when I can reflect on how my life in each day has been guided, when I recognise that I have come through situations beyond my own strength. In my Bible I have several bookmarks; one is the ancient prayer of Patrick: 'Christ with me, Christ before me, Christ behind me, Christ within me.' I need this reminder that there is nothing I have to face in my own strength. Christ is not only with me but, in the miracle of eternity, touching my soul from within. What a thought!

Lord, you know my deepest need. You are my strength this day and always.

ELIZABETH RUNDLE

Friday 13 September   **1 John 4:9–12 (NIV)**

The miracle of indwelling love

This is how God showed his love among us: he sent his one and only Son into the world that we might live through him. This is love: not that we loved God, but that he loved us and sent his Son as an atoning sacrifice for our sins. Dear friends, since God so loved us, we also ought to love one another. No one has ever seen God; but if we love one another, God lives in us and his love is made complete in us.

Writing letters seems to be a thing of the past, with the pen now replaced by all the various forms of social media. Nevertheless, the purpose of communication remains the same as it ever was, even though it is now more immediate. We post, we tweet, we WhatsApp and we Skype in order to share with friends the most important thing on our minds or the high point of our day. With that in mind, letters from some of the first Christian leaders enable us to identify their most important message for their far-away followers.

In today's message, John writes about a truth that comforted and inspired him over his long life, a truth he felt was vital to pass on – we frail humans, however fragmented, rudderless or despairing, are restored and made whole by God's indwelling love.

And isn't it marvellous that we, some 2,000 years from John's original letter, are receiving the message as if it was just to us? These short verses, usually swallowed by the rest of the chapter, are staggering in their simplicity. The idea of God's living *in* us is simple to say, but it is a concept so amazing that it is beyond our understanding.

The good news is I don't need to understand this to believe it! I put my trust in this miracle of love, this miracle of a relationship through Jesus with the almighty and creating God. It is both a relationship and a communication to enrich all our relationships and enable us to communicate empathy and compassion. In other words, our lives are meant to share the great love of God with others.

What would you consider to be the most important aspect of your faith to communicate to those you love?

ELIZABETH RUNDLE

Vision of the kingdom of God

I saw the Holy City, the new Jerusalem, coming down out of heaven from God, prepared as a bride beautifully dressed for her husband. And I heard a loud voice from the throne saying, 'Look! God's dwelling-place is now among the people, and he will dwell with them. They will be his people, and God himself will be with them and be their God. "He will wipe every tear from their eyes. There will be no more death" or mourning or crying or pain, for the old order of things has passed away.'

Over the past two weeks we have dipped into the Bible, tracing God's specific and intimate promises from Genesis to today's verses in the book of Revelation. The word of God has been given to individuals and communities and, in mystery and miracle, we receive the promise and the actuality of that presence in our own lives. Here we bring the beacon promises to their zenith. As the anonymous writer of Hebrews put it, 'Jesus Christ is the same yesterday and today and forever' (Hebrews 13:8).

Imagine for a moment that you are looking down on an airport runway. On each side of the runway you can see lights studded into the tarmac to keep the planes safely on course. Now imagine the 66 books of the Bible placed individually and flat to form a runway. The beacon promises we have looked at (and there are many more) become the lights by which Christians find their secure direction through life. As life's journey progresses and we approach the end of our runway, we place our trust for eternity in the saving grace of God's presence in Jesus Christ.

And what a vision we have of 'eternity'! The fulfilment of the kingdom of God, the restoration of relationship with the creator of all things seen and unseen. No more mourning, crying or pain. We lift off into the everlasting arms of love.

When Revd John Wesley (1703–91), founder of Methodism, was dying, he murmured, 'The best of all is, God is with us.' The Word made flesh, God's supreme promise, dwells among and within you and me. May we take time each day to recognise this gift of love.

'Forever with the Lord. Amen, so let it be' (James Montgomery, 1771–1854).

ELIZABETH RUNDLE

Introduction

Success and failure

The words 'success' and 'failure' do not appear anywhere in the Bible – they are modern concepts – but I think we have many Bible stories of people, individually or as a nation, succeeding or failing in their enterprises. God's view, however, of what constitutes a success or a failure might be very different from ours. In the books of Kings, for instance, monarchs are classified not by whether they made the economy flourish or extended the borders of the nation, but by whether they 'did what was right in the eyes of the Lord' or 'did what was evil in the sight of the Lord'. Faithfulness to God's commands does not ensure power or privilege, and those who do wrong are not always punished, at least at the time.

In the New Testament, in particular, Jesus and then his disciple Paul seem completely to reverse society's ideas of success and failure. Jesus refers to his coming humiliating death as 'the hour… for the Son of Man to be glorified' (John 12:23, NRSV), while Paul later boasts not of how many churches he has planted, but of how many trials, arrests, beatings and shipwrecks he has gone through in his missionary endeavours (e.g. 2 Corinthians 11:23–29).

In our daily lives, do we seek to fulfil our ambitions, or rather to be faithful to God's calling? We do not have to be rich or famous to be 'successful' in God's eyes; many whom the world sees as failures may turn out to be heroes and heroines when the kingdom comes. Meanwhile, in the prophecy of Mary, who like all prophets speaks as though the events have already happened, God 'has brought down the powerful from their thrones, and lifted up the lowly; he has filled the hungry with good things, and sent the rich away empty' (Luke 1:52–53, NRSV).

I have chosen to pursue these two themes through the Bible chronologically, to give an overview of scripture's handling of them. Throughout the Bible, I have found that often, apparent success is really failure and apparent failure, really success.

VERONICA ZUNDEL

O happy fault?

They heard the sound of the Lord God walking in the garden at the time of the evening breeze, and the man and his wife hid themselves from the presence of the Lord God among the trees of the garden. But the Lord God called to the man, and said to him, 'Where are you?' He said, 'I heard the sound of you in the garden, and I was afraid, because I was naked; and I hid myself.' He said, 'Who told you that you were naked? Have you eaten from the tree of which I commanded you not to eat?'

When she was already in her 90s, my late mother read the classic children's book *Pollyanna* for the first time. In the book, Pollyanna plays the 'Glad Game', in which she finds a blessing in every difficult circumstance. For instance, when the 'missionary box' yielded her a pair of crutches instead of a doll, she was glad that she didn't need them. My mother, who was a bit of a Pollyanna herself, loved it. Even though she had lost her birth family through the persecution of Jews in Poland, her adoptive family in the Holocaust and her only son to suicide, on her deathbed she could still say, 'I've been very lucky.' And she wasn't even a Christian.

In a similar way, medieval theologians referred to 'the fall' described in Genesis 3 as 'O felix culpa!' (O happy fault), since it led to Jesus' becoming human to save us from sin. It's hard to think of human wrongdoing as in any way a good thing, but we can still rejoice in the fact that God comes to us in the midst of all our failures, and has the capacity to redeem our biggest mess-ups and turn them to good purposes. The apostle Paul tells us that 'all things work together for good for those who love God, who are called according to his purpose' (Romans 8:28). He doesn't mean that our every problem will be solved, but that God can create good out of anything that happens to us or that we, mistakenly or deliberately, do – even our deepest failure.

'Even though you intended to do harm to me, God intended it for good' (Genesis 50:20).

VERONICA ZUNDEL

Monday 16 September — Genesis 4:19, 23–24 (NRSV)

A real man

Lamech took two wives; the name of one was Adah, and the name of the other Zillah… Lamech said to his wives: 'Adah and Zillah, hear my voice; you wives of Lamech, listen to what I say: I have killed a man for wounding me, a young man for striking me. If Cain is avenged sevenfold, truly Lamech seventy-sevenfold.'

Just one chapter after we have seen the beginning of human sin, this ancient story shows how quickly and how far evil spreads in the world. Already Lamech is treating women as commodities, accumulating wives to show his power; and now he boasts of his own violence and thirst for revenge. We should always remember that the command 'An eye for an eye' (Matthew 5:38; see also Exodus 21:24) is about limiting violence, preventing it from escalating. It is a provision, not a prescription. Lamech's boast shows how dangerous unlimited violence can be.

Lamech appears to be what many would think of as 'a real man': someone who stands up for himself, who attracts women by his strength, who won't put up with any insult. He could be seen in worldly terms as a success. Certainly many of our film heroes seem to be modelled on him! But is this really what God has called men to?

This passage, with its threat of 'seventy-sevenfold' revenge, brings to mind how Jesus used the same calculation in telling Peter how often to forgive: 'Then Peter came and said to him, "Lord, if another member of the church sins against me, how often should I forgive? As many as seven times?" Jesus said to him, "Not seven times, but, I tell you, seventy-seven times"' (Matthew 18:21–22). Surely Jesus had Lamech's story in mind as he said this. Christian forgiveness reverses the violence that pervades society and 'disarms' the powers of oppression and conflict.

As disciples of Jesus, we have a different idea of success from that of the rest of our society. Events and circumstances that look to the world like failure may in fact be our greatest successes in discipleship, because of how they shape us into the image of Christ.

'I am for peace; but when I speak, they are for war' (Psalm 120:7).

VERONICA ZUNDEL

Tuesday 17 September   Genesis 16:7–10, 13 (NRSV, abridged)

At the lowest point

The angel of the Lord found [Hagar] by a spring of water in the wilderness, the spring on the way to Shur. And he said, 'Hagar, slave-girl of Sarai, where have you come from and where are you going?' She said, 'I am running away from my mistress Sarai.' The angel of the Lord said to her, 'Return to your mistress, and submit to her.' The angel of the Lord also said to her, 'I will so greatly multiply your offspring that they cannot be counted for multitude'... So she named the Lord who spoke to her, 'You are El-roi'; for she said, 'Have I really seen God and remained alive after seeing him?'

I have a fondness for Hagar, as for other strong biblical women who fought against their limited destiny. She had no real choice about bearing Abram's child, and all it earned her was ill-treatment from Sarai (admittedly she had mocked Sarai's infertility; see Genesis 16:4). For a female runaway slave, practically the only options were destitution or prostitution.

Here she is at one of her two lowest points in the story: pregnant and alone in the desert, with nowhere to go. Yet this is where God meets her, and where she becomes the first person in the Bible to give a new name to God: El-Roi, meaning 'the God who sees me'.

When we are in despair, lonely, disappointed with life, perhaps in real danger, Hagar's story reminds us that God sees our situation and is with us. Hagar was an Egyptian, not one of God's people; yet God assures her that she too has an important role in history, a future and a hope. In the meantime, she is to submit to her circumstances as Sarai's servant, until God's time to call her out of that difficult role. I don't think this command means that we must always accept oppression (for instance, by staying in an abusive marriage). It does tell us that sometimes we have to stay with our failures to find God's way of success – to rest in the darkness until we begin to see light.

Pray for anyone you know who is at a low point. Perhaps it's yourself.

VERONICA ZUNDEL

Wednesday 18 September   **Exodus 15:19–21 (NRSV)**

Celebrating success

When the horses of Pharaoh with his chariots and his chariot drivers went into the sea, the Lord brought back the waters of the sea upon them; but the Israelites walked through the sea on dry ground. Then the prophet Miriam, Aaron's sister, took a tambourine in her hand; and all the women went out after her with tambourines and with dancing. And Miriam sang to them: 'Sing to the Lord, for he has triumphed gloriously; horse and rider he has thrown into the sea.'

If you use social media, do you sometimes get jaded at people posting news of their children's academic success or their latest wonderful holiday? I must confess I do. It's so easy to start comparing my own life with their apparently perfect lives (though, of course, we don't see all the problems they don't post).

Miriam is celebrating not her own victory, but that of God's people – or perhaps more accurately, God's victory on behalf of God's people. Music and dancing are common to all humanity as a way of marking good times: a wedding, a reunion, the birth of a baby or a book. Yet the Jewish people have a way of remembering that what was victory for the Hebrew slaves, was defeat for the Egyptian masters. In the Passover meal, there is a point where the guests recite all the ten plagues of Egypt, for each plague dipping a finger into their wineglass and letting a drop of wine fall on to their plate. With this ritual they acknowledge that there are losers as well as winners in their sacred history.

It is right and good to rejoice in blessings that come to us. Ecclesiastes puts it like this: 'There is nothing better for mortals than to eat and drink, and find enjoyment in their toil' (Ecclesiastes 2:24). In our worship, too, there is always a place for praise and thanksgiving. Yet we should also think of those who are excluded from our celebration, for whom it is perhaps a painful reminder of sorrow: the childless couple at an infant baptism or dedication, for example, or the parents of a learning-disabled child at a graduation.

How can we allow both celebration and lament in our church life?

VERONICA ZUNDEL

Thursday 19 September — Exodus 17:11–13 (NRSV)

Success by teamwork

Whenever Moses held up his hand, Israel prevailed; and whenever he lowered his hand, Amalek prevailed. But Moses' hands grew weary; so they took a stone and put it under him, and he sat on it. Aaron and Hur held up his hands, one on one side, and the other on the other side; so his hands were steady until the sun set. And Joshua defeated Amalek and his people with the sword.

We live in an individualistic society, and our faith sometimes risks becoming individualistic too. Just as the world around us wants heroes, we adulate our Christian heroes, past and present. Yet which of them actually achieved whatever they achieved without the prayers, financial backing and moral support supplied by other Christians?

Moses is one of our ultimate Christian heroes. But he too, didn't get the children of Israel out of Egypt and through their 40 years of wandering in the desert, surrounded by hostile tribes, on his own. His brother Aaron and sister Miriam, as well as other leaders of the people, helped to make it all happen. And in this story, Moses is himself a helper too: as he prays, supported by two 'handholders', so Joshua fights and wins the battle.

Today we Christians are called to fight spiritual, not physical, battles: 'For our struggle is not against enemies of blood and flesh, but against the rulers, against the authorities, against the cosmic powers of this present darkness, against the spiritual forces of evil in the heavenly places' (Ephesians 6:12). Theologian Walter Wink has written with much insight about the influence of 'the powers' as embodied today in corporations or political entities. Our 'weapons', therefore, are spiritual: prayer, Christlike attitudes, and above all love for one another, so that we may fight hatred, greed and violence together. The life of discipleship must be a life in community, however we express and build that, or we will always fail in our endeavours.

'Put on the whole armour of God, that you may be able to stand against the wiles of the devil' (Ephesians 6:11).

VERONICA ZUNDEL

Friday 20 September   Judges 7:2–5, 7 (NRSV, abridged)

Less is more

The Lord said to Gideon, 'The troops with you are too many for me to give the Midianites into their hand. Israel would only take the credit away from me, saying, "My own hand has delivered me." Now therefore proclaim this in the hearing of the troops, "Whoever is fearful and trembling, let him return home."' Thus Gideon sifted them out; twenty-two thousand returned, and ten thousand remained. Then the Lord said to Gideon, 'The troops are still too many; take them down to the water and I will sift them out for you there'... So he brought the troops down to the water; and the Lord said to Gideon, 'All those who lap the water with their tongues, as a dog laps, you shall put to one side; all those who kneel down to drink, putting their hands to their mouths, you shall put to the other side'... Then the Lord said to Gideon, 'With the three hundred that lapped I will deliver you, and give the Midianites into your hand...'

Today's reading might seem to say the opposite to yesterday's. God is asking Gideon to accept less help. Actually the lesson of both is the same: any success is ultimately God's doing, not ours.

I have a problem when 'successful' people say, 'I give God all the glory.' Sometimes it feels like they are saying, 'Look how humble I am.' In reality our every enterprise is a cooperation between us and God: God wants us to use our inbuilt, God-given abilities. So Gideon goes to battle not with no troops at all, but with a highly inadequate army. With God, even a little is enough.

Mennonite scholar Millard Lind, in his book *Yahweh is a Warrior* (Herald Press, 1987), explores how God instructed the Israelites not to acquire the latest military technology, such as horses and chariots. This was to demonstrate that God was fighting on their behalf, and that ultimately it was the power of God, not the force of arms, that brought victory.

'When they bring you before the synagogues, the rulers and the authorities, do not worry about how you are to defend yourselves or what you are to say; for the Holy Spirit will teach you at that very hour what you ought to say' (Luke 12:11–12).

VERONICA ZUNDEL

Saturday 21 September — 2 Samuel 7:1–5, 7, 12–13 (NRSV, abridged)

The limits of success

Now when the king was settled in his house, and the Lord had given him rest from all his enemies around him, the king said to the prophet Nathan, 'See now, I am living in a house of cedar, but the ark of God stays in a tent.' Nathan said to the king, 'Go, do all that you have in mind; for the Lord is with you.' But that same night the word of the Lord came to Nathan: Go and tell my servant David: Thus says the Lord: Are you the one to build me a house to live in?... Wherever I have moved about among all the people of Israel, did I ever speak a word with any of the tribal leaders of Israel... saying, 'Why have you not built me a house of cedar?'... I will raise up your offspring after you, who shall come forth from your body... He shall build a house for my name, and I will establish the throne of his kingdom forever.

One of my fellow students on my MA course in writing poetry said, 'I know at my age I'm never going to have a great poetry career; I just want to be a better amateur poet.' I admire his realism. 'I can do all things through him who strengthens me' (Philippians 4:13) does not mean 'You can do anything if you believe enough.' Rather, it means that God will give us strength to do whatever God has called us to do.

David had 'shed much blood' (1 Chronicles 22:8) – he had attained the throne by violence, and although he was also called by God to be king, his violent history barred him from building a temple to the God of peace. He could only leave it to his son Solomon to build the temple after David's death. Wisely, David accepts this limitation on his achievements as king. We too may have to accept our own limitations. Stories of Christian celebrities can do us a disservice, by giving us unrealistic expectations: we will not all be 'Christian stars' but we can fulfil our own potential under God. And who knows what legacy we may leave?

As often observed, God calls us to faithfulness, not success.

VERONICA ZUNDEL

Sunday 22 September **1 Kings 19:1–4 (NRSV)**

A fall comes after pride

Ahab told Jezebel all that Elijah had done, and how he had killed all the prophets with the sword. Then Jezebel sent a messenger to Elijah, saying, 'So may the gods do to me, and more also, if I do not make your life like the life of one of them by this time tomorrow.' Then he was afraid; he got up and fled for his life, and came to Beer-sheba, which belongs to Judah; he left his servant there. But he himself went a day's journey into the wilderness, and came and sat down under a solitary broom tree. He asked that he might die: 'It is enough; now, O Lord, take away my life, for I am no better than my ancestors.'

My late mother had a German saying that roughly translates as 'Nothing is harder to bear than a series of wonderful days.' For many of us, a big triumph is often followed by a huge low. Just as Elijah has witnessed a massive victory for Israel's God over Baal, the god of Canaan, he slumps into depression so severe that he wants to die. Of course, Jezebel's threats might be a factor, but surely after Mount Carmel, he knows God can be trusted? Apparently not.

Do we too look only at the things we got wrong and not those that went right? I know that after giving a talk I always dwell on the things I wish I had remembered to say, and those I wish I hadn't said. Perhaps it is at these times that we most need the honest appraisal of others around us, who can look at what we have done dispassionately and tell us not only what needs changing, but also what deserves praise.

Right after this low point, God speaks to Elijah clearly, not in a dramatic wind, earthquake or fire, but in a barely audible voice. God tells Elijah exactly whom to anoint as king and who will be Elijah's own successor. In other words, Elijah sees that he is not alone, and that he will not have to bear the burden of being a prophet forever.

God sometimes speaks to us more clearly in our pain
than in our happiness.

VERONICA ZUNDEL

Monday 23 September   **Matthew 14:28–31 (NRSV)**

The danger of overconfidence

Peter answered him, 'Lord, if it is you, command me to come to you on the water. He said, 'Come.' So Peter got out of the boat, started walking on the water, and came towards Jesus. But when he noticed the strong wind, he became frightened, and beginning to sink, he cried out, 'Lord, save me!' Jesus immediately reached out his hand and caught him, saying to him, 'You of little faith, why did you doubt?'

My husband, bless him, claims that he only ever makes a mistake once. This may be true of his work, but it certainly isn't true domestically. Sometimes I have to tell him over and over where a particular item is stored! I, on the other hand, know that I make the same mistakes for years, even decades, before I learn from them. I wouldn't dare to boast that I learn from a single mistake.

Peter seems to start with more confidence in himself than he has in Jesus – note the 'if it is you'. We have to commend his desire to imitate Jesus, but as soon as things get a bit scary, he loses all his bravado and starts sinking. He seems to have forgotten that 'Do not be afraid' is not only an oft-repeated saying of Jesus, but one of the most common commands in the whole Bible. Fear is one of the biggest factors in stopping us venturing out and taking risks for God.

Self-belief is one component of success, at least in worldly terms, but faith in God's power to save us is far more important. The 17th-century mystic Brother Lawrence had a lame leg and often stumbled in his household tasks, such as delivering wine casks to the monastery's customers. When this happened, or he made some other mistake, he would say to God, 'If it weren't for you, I would be doing this all the time.' I find that a wise way to look at our own failings. Without God, we are of precious little use, even if we have great gifts. Only under God's guidance can we use them effectively, in the service of love.

'There is no fear in love, but perfect love casts out fear' (1 John 4:18).

VERONICA ZUNDEL

Tuesday 24 September   **Luke 12:16–20 (NRSV)**

Success is fragile

Then he told them a parable: 'The land of a rich man produced abundantly. And he thought to himself, "What should I do, for I have no place to store my crops?" Then he said, "I will do this: I will pull down my barns and build larger ones, and there I will store all my grain and my goods. And I will say to my soul, Soul, you have ample goods laid up for many years; relax, eat, drink, be merry." But God said to him, "You fool! This very night your life is being demanded of you. And the things you have prepared, whose will they be?"'

The tale is told of a visitor to Holland who spoke no Dutch but asked everyone in his own language what he was seeing. 'Who owns this big house?' he would ask, and the Dutch would reply, 'Kan niet verstaan' ('I don't understand'). Then he would ask, 'Whose flashy car is that?' and hear the same answer. 'This man Kannietverstaan must be very rich and powerful,' he thought. Finally, he saw a funeral procession and asked a stranger whose body was in the coffin. 'Kan niet verstaan' was the reply. 'Ah,' thought the tourist, 'even such a great man as Kannietverstaan cannot escape death.'

Financial or even artistic or scientific success is fleeting. Jesus tells us later in this chapter not to store up treasures on earth, but to accumulate treasures in heaven. What does this mean? I think it means that when we die, leaving behind memories of our kindness and generosity will be worth more than leaving behind a tax-free inheritance for any children we have. This strikes particularly hard for those of us in the rich west who have so much. Perhaps this is why Jesus says, 'Blessed are the poor,' for they know they have nothing to hand on but love. We need not so much to declutter our houses, as to fill our lives with acts of goodness towards others. That is the kind of hoarding that will leave no headaches for our heirs.

'Do not seek what you are to eat and what you are to drink… Seek [God's] kingdom, and these things will be added to you' (Luke 12:29, 31, ESV).

VERONICA ZUNDEL

Wednesday 25 September Mark 15:33–34, 37–39 (NRSV)

The power of failure

When it was noon, darkness came over the whole land until three in the afternoon. At three o'clock Jesus cried out with a loud voice, 'Eloi, Eloi, lema sabachthani?' which means, 'My God, my God, why have you forsaken me?'… Then Jesus gave a loud cry and breathed his last. And the curtain of the temple was torn in two, from top to bottom. Now when the centurion, who stood facing him, saw that in this way he breathed his last, he said, 'Truly this man was God's Son!'

The death of Christ could be seen as the greatest failure in human history. Here is a man who declares that he has come to usher in the kingdom of God, a new world where justice and peace will reign; and he ends his life in his early 30s, executed as a common criminal, and almost all his followers have fled (the women stayed).

We have the power of hindsight: we know about the resurrection, God's proof that not even death can conquer sacrificial love. But the Roman centurion did not have this advantage. What convinced him that Jesus was the revelation of God's nature, the image of his Father, and just when Jesus had apparently felt forsaken by God?

I think it must have been something in the quality of the way Jesus met his death. We know from the other gospels that he did not struggle to hold on to life. Instead he committed his spirit into God's hands, so that the soldiers who came to inspect him did not have to break his legs to stop him being able to push himself up to breathe. Was this what impressed the centurion?

This raises an intriguing possibility. What if it is in the way we accept our failures, rather than in our successes, that others will see the presence of God in and among us? What if we don't have to demonstrate what good Christians we are before we can witness to our faith? Perhaps it is our very fallibility, and our conviction that God loves us infinitely in the face of it, that will shine out as a beacon of God's grace and forgiveness.

Pray that God will be visible even through your failures.

VERONICA ZUNDEL

Thursday 26 September Luke 23:39–43 (NRSV)

Undeserved success

One of the criminals who were hanged there kept deriding him and saying, 'Are you not the Messiah? Save yourself and us!' But the other rebuked him, saying, 'Do you not fear God, since you are under the same sentence of condemnation? And we indeed have been condemned justly, for we are getting what we deserve for our deeds, but this man has done nothing wrong.' Then he said, 'Jesus, remember me when you come into your kingdom.' He replied, 'Truly I tell you, today you will be with me in Paradise.'

I read recently of a clergyman who wanted to determine who was worthy and who was unworthy, so that he could withhold communion from the unworthy. I think he's got it all wrong. The apostle Paul makes it clear in 1 Corinthians that while we should examine our consciences before partaking, the only qualification for eating the bread and drinking the cup is that we should 'discern the body' – that is, recognise the presence of Christ in this sharing and in each other. On this measure, the repentant criminal has got it right: he recognises the presence of God in Jesus and throws himself on Christ's mercy.

The result is that Jesus accepts the criminal's faith and promises him salvation: not just a 'ticket to heaven' but a transformation of his life, even after death, and a place with Jesus in the undeserved love of God. In life, the criminal was a failure: he chose wrongly, and he wasn't even good enough at crime to get away without punishment. But next to Jesus, he receives a 'success' he never dreamed of, the chance to live forever in the presence of the one who has loved him from the beginning.

Sometimes life offers us a joy or an opportunity that we would never have expected, and it can come even when we think our life is over. All we need to do is be ready for it and accept it. An attitude of defiance and cynicism, like that of the first criminal, will only condemn us to futility. Being open to God's leading may bring joyful surprises into our life.

'Jesus, remember me when you come into your kingdom':
make this your prayer today.

VERONICA ZUNDEL

Friday 27 September   **2 Corinthians 11:30; 12:7b–9a (NRSV)**

Reverse boasting

If I must boast, I will boast of the things that show my weakness… To keep me from being too elated, a thorn was given me in the flesh, a messenger of Satan to torment me, to keep me from being too elated. Three times I appealed to the Lord about this, that it would leave me, but he said to me, 'My grace is sufficient for you, for power is made perfect in weakness.'

'Christ Jesus came into the world to save sinners – of whom I am the foremost', writes Paul in his first letter to Timothy (1 Timothy 1:15). This always makes me laugh; I get the feeling Paul was a man who had to be top at everything, even sinning! Elsewhere, as in today's reading, he makes it quite clear that his weakness is the only thing he is prepared to boast about. To get the Corinthians to listen, he will not throw his weight about and emphasise his authority, but only remind them of how, in Christ, God has forgiven even him, the former persecutor of the church.

Many translations render verse 9 as 'my power is made perfect in weakness'. I have even heard it as 'my power is perfect in your weakness'. But neither 'my' nor 'your' appears in the original Greek. What we have here is not an abusive God who most displays his own power when we are weakest, but rather a universal spiritual law, that the greatest manifestation of power is to be able to be weak and vulnerable.

This is what Jesus demonstrated on the cross, and it should be the principle for our relations with each other as Christians, and with the world we serve. Under this law, success becomes failure, and failure success. But in a society that worships strength, fame and wealth, this is not easy to remember. Even in the church, we are prone to give most attention to those who appear most 'successful' in their Christian life, when in fact God may be most interested in obscure but faithful disciples.

'You know that those who are considered rulers of the Gentiles lord it over them, and their great ones exercise authority over them. But it shall not be so among you' (Mark 10:42–43a, ESV).

VERONICA ZUNDEL

Saturday 28 September — Revelation 20:4, 6b (NRSV)

The route to success

Then I saw thrones, and those seated on them were given authority to judge. I also saw the souls of those who had been beheaded for their testimony to Jesus and for the word of God. They had not worshipped the beast or its image and had not received its mark on their foreheads or their hands. They came to life and reigned with Christ for a thousand years… Over these the second death has no power, but they will be priests of God and of Christ, and they will reign with him a thousand years.

Didn't Jesus tell us not to judge others (Luke 6:37)? Yet here are martyrs for their faith being given authority to judge the world. I think the difference is that now we are fallible, ill-equipped to judge others since we ourselves are liable to judgement. In the new creation, however, we will be transformed into the likeness of Christ, and have Christ's authority to distinguish good from evil.

However you interpret the 'thousand years' in today's passage, this picture of the people of God reigning for a millennium is a great inspiration to seek Christlikeness, so that we will be ready for the task. This gives us no authority to rule over others now – far from it. Rather, we should humbly try to promote good in the world, without condemning those who don't share our values.

This is true success: not that we disapprove of or shun others, but that we put all our efforts, with the aid of the Holy Spirit, in helping to create the renewed, peaceful and just world that is to come. God can do this without us but instead has chosen to do it with us.

On the way, there will almost certainly be suffering – the martyrs described here have paid the ultimate price for their stance for God, and some people still do today. God's way of success is not a primrose path to prominence; it passes through the valley of the shadow of death.

'Let us run with perseverance the race that is set before us, looking to Jesus the pioneer and perfecter of our faith, who for the sake of the joy that was set before him endured the cross' (Hebrews 12:1–2).

VERONICA ZUNDEL

Introduction

Francis and Clare

It wasn't Francis or Clare who first drew me to become a Franciscan. It was the experience of spending time with people living a Franciscan life. Over the 30-plus years since, however, Francis and Clare have stepped out of their medieval past and become very real to me. Francis was born around 1182 and died in 1226; Clare, a little younger, was born around 1193 and died in 1253. They lived in Umbria, central Italy, in the town of Assisi.

From their very different world, they have become friends, companions, guides and inspirations for my own Franciscan life. I've found connections between their lives and my own, and I've read their writings (which is quite manageable – neither wrote much) and the stories that those who knew them recorded.

Their world, like mine, was full of wars and rumours of wars. Small city states fought against one another, emperors and popes fell out, and the Crusades were taking place, pitting Christian against Muslim. Francis and Clare struggled to make peace and to sustain it among all this aggression.

I've been inspired by Francis' example of preaching and mission, his deep desire to share his own experience of faith with others, and equally inspired as my own more contemplative vocation has developed by the example of Clare and her burning commitment to prayer. As I trained for the priesthood, I found encouragement in the great value both placed on the Eucharist, and their desire for their followers to share that reverence.

Francis sometimes struggled to discern his calling, and in particular what he felt as a tension between serving others in active ministry and the prayer which undergirded it all. I've seen something of my own struggle over the years mirrored in his.

As I've been given responsibility within my Franciscan community, I've drawn on the wisdom of Francis and Clare in their own leadership. They faced struggles to be accepted by a divided church, and problems with differing and apparently incompatible visions among their members, which are certainly not confined to their own time. They have given me courage to keep on in my own leadership.

I hope in this fortnight you will come to value these two saints as I do, and will be enriched by their lives and example.

HELEN JULIAN CSF

Sunday 29 September   **John 21:15–17 (NRSV)**

A sense of the divine

When they had finished breakfast, Jesus said to Simon Peter, 'Simon son of John, do you love me more than these?' He said to him, 'Yes, Lord; you know that I love you.' Jesus said to him, 'Feed my lambs.' A second time he said to him, 'Simon son of John, do you love me?' He said to him, 'Yes, Lord; you know that I love you.' Jesus said to him, 'Tend my sheep.' He said to him the third time, 'Simon, son of John, do you love me?' Peter felt hurt because he said to him the third time, 'Do you love me?' And he said to him, 'Lord, you know everything; you know that I love you.' Jesus said to him, 'Feed my sheep.'

God's calling can come anywhere, and often more than once. To Peter this calling came on a beach; to Francis one of the key callings came in a deserted church.

The ruined church of San Damiano lies a little below Assisi. There was a striking crucifix there and Francis was drawn to spending time praying in front of it. As he did, it seemed that the figure of Jesus spoke to him, saying, 'Francis, go and repair my house, which, as you see, is falling completely into ruin.'

Francis responded immediately. He began to gather stones together and to repair the church. When he needed more resources, he sold some of the cloth from his father's business and used the proceeds.

Our own callings will not always be as clear as this one. We need to listen for God's voice through the events of our lives, and be prepared to act on what we believe we hear, but also go on listening as God continues to speak and to call.

This is the prayer Francis used before the crucifix; you may find it powerful to use it yourself as you seek God's calling in your life: 'Most High and glorious God, enlighten the darkness of our hearts and give us a true faith, a certain hope and a perfect love. Give us a sense of the divine and knowledge of yourself, so that we may do everything in fulfilment of your holy will, through Jesus Christ our Lord.'

HELEN JULIAN CSF

Monday 30 September — Matthew 10:34–38 (NRSV)

Hard choices

[Jesus said,] 'Do not think that I have come to bring peace to the earth; I have not come to bring peace, but a sword. For I have come to set a man against his father, and a daughter against her mother, and a daughter-in-law against her mother-in-law; and one's foes will be members of one's own household. Whoever loves father or mother more than me is not worthy of me; and whoever loves son or daughter more than me is not worthy of me; and whoever does not take up the cross and follow me is not worthy of me.'

Francis' father did not take his sale of the cloth well, or peaceably. In fact, he dragged Francis before the bishop of Assisi and demanded the return of the money. Francis, in a dramatic gesture, returned not only the money, but also the clothes off his back, and swore that in future he would have only one father, his Father in heaven.

Clare, a young woman from a noble family, heard Francis preaching and was inspired to make a dramatic break with her own family. She left her home in secret on the night of Palm Sunday 1212, and met Francis and the small group of men who had joined him. Together they went to a small church, the Portiuncula, on the plain below Assisi, where Clare changed her rich dress for a simple habit, and Francis cut her hair. Clare, joined by her sister Agnes, began a new life at San Damiano. Clare was only 18, and she lived there until she died.

Unlike Francis' family, Clare's came to accept her way of life, and in fact another sister and her mother joined the community at San Damiano.

Family is important, but God's calling is more important. In the gospel, Jesus challenges the primacy of family, and Francis and Clare lived out these words. Of course, there may be other things that prevent you from hearing and following God – it may be career, status or security. But family ties have a particular strength, and family is held as very important today.

Can you recall a time when you had to choose between family and God's calling? How did you decide and which did you choose?

HELEN JULIAN CSF

Tuesday 1 October   **Genesis 1:24–27 (NRSV)**

Creator and creation

And God said, 'Let the earth bring forth living creatures of every kind: cattle and creeping things and wild animals of the earth of every kind.' And it was so. God made the wild animals of the earth of every kind, and the cattle of every kind, and everything that creeps upon the ground of every kind. And God saw that it was good. Then God said, 'Let us make humankind in our image, according to our likeness; and let them have dominion over the fish of the sea, and over the birds of the air, and over the cattle, and over all the wild animals of the earth, and over every creeping thing that creeps upon the earth.' So God created humankind in his image, in the image of God he created them; male and female he created them.

If you know anything at all about Francis, it's probably that he loved animals. Although it's not the whole story, it is true. Francis and Clare shared a love, compassion and respect for all creatures, human and non-human. Their sense of family extended to the whole of creation; all shared the one creator and Father, and therefore everyone and everything was brother and sister. Francis expressed this most strikingly in his 'Canticle of the Creatures', which you may have sung as 'All Creatures of our God and King'. The sun and fire are brothers, the moon and water are sisters, and all are called upon to praise God for their being.

God made creatures of every kind, and saw that they were good. If we are to follow Francis and Clare, we need to praise God for the spider in the corner of the room as well as the cat videos that make us smile. And we also need to remember the creator, the giver of these gifts of creation. Just as we try to love our difficult cousin as well as our favourite aunt, so we need to praise God for all of creation, because all is part of our family.

Perhaps today you could spend some time giving thanks for the parts of creation you don't naturally see as 'good'? Bring them to mind, and find something to give thanks to God for in each of them.

HELEN JULIAN CSF

Wednesday 2 October   **Matthew 14:15–20a (NRSV)**

Making much out of little

When it was evening, the disciples came to [Jesus] and said, 'This is a deserted place, and the hour is now late; send the crowds away so that they may go into the villages and buy food for themselves.' Jesus said to them, 'They need not go away; you give them something to eat.' They replied, 'We have nothing here but five loaves and two fish.' And he said, 'Bring them here to me.' Then he ordered the crowds to sit down on the grass. Taking the five loaves and the two fish, he looked up to heaven, and blessed and broke the loaves, and gave them to the disciples, and the disciples gave them to the crowds. And all ate and were filled.

Jesus saw the need of the crowds around him, and made five loaves and two fish into enough food to feed them all. Clare's community grew rapidly as women were inspired by her way of life and came to join her. They were committed to poverty, as was Francis, and for Clare and her sisters this sometimes meant not having enough to eat.

One day, when the sisters were seated in the refectory for their lunch, there was only half a loaf of bread to share between them. Clare told Cecilia to cut 50 slices from it. Her reply shows the down-to-earth relationship of Clare to her sisters: 'The Lord's miracle of loaves and fishes would be needed to get 50 slices out of that!' But she obeyed Clare, and cut 50 'large and good slices', so that all the sisters were fed.

Where most of us would see only what was lacking, as the disciples did, Jesus, and Clare, trusted that God would provide. Both stories challenge us to believe that God does care for our needs. But we are not to sit back and just wait for God to act; we're also challenged to believe that the little we can offer will, with the help of God, be enough, and more than enough.

God of the loaves and fishes, may we be moved to action by the needs of others, and offer what we have, so that all may be fed in your name.

HELEN JULIAN CSF

Thursday 3 October — John 14:23–24, 27 (NRSV)

May the Lord give you peace

Jesus [said], 'Those who love me will keep my word, and my Father will love them, and we will come to them and make our home with them. Whoever does not love me does not keep my words; and the word that you hear is not mine, but is from the Father who sent me… Peace I leave with you; my peace I give to you. I do not give as the world gives. Do not let your hearts be troubled, and do not let them be afraid.'

In the *Testament*, which he wrote near the end of his life, Francis recalled that the Lord had revealed to him a greeting, 'May the Lord give you peace.' And in his life, he did his best to bring peace where there was conflict.

One of the best-known stories from the life of Francis is that of the wolf of Gubbio. The people of Gubbio were being terrorised by a large and hungry wolf, who stole their sheep. They even feared for their children. When Francis heard of this, he went to Gubbio and offered to mediate between the people and the wolf. They feared he would be eaten alive, but he went out anyway, and greeted the wolf with respect, calling him brother. Then he led him back to the town, where the wolf agreed, by putting his paw into Francis' hand, that he would stop terrorising the people, and the people agreed that they would feed the wolf.

Making peace takes courage. And it also requires a willingness to see both sides of a conflict and to understand why peace has broken down. A true peacemaker must win the trust of both sides, so that they are willing to move out of the familiarity of their conflict and to trust that a new relationship of peace is possible. It can be daunting, but once again Jesus tells us not to fear. As he supplies our material needs, he also gives his peace. And, as with all his gifts, we are to share this peace.

Reflecting on the words of Jesus, and the story of Francis and the wolf of Gubbio, how might you be a peacemaker in a situation of conflict in your life – in your family, at work, at church?

HELEN JULIAN CSF

Friday 4 October   **Luke 12:29–34 (NRSV)**

Poverty and generosity

And do not keep striving for what you are to eat and what you are to drink, and do not keep worrying. For it is the nations of the world that strive after all these things, and your Father knows that you need them. Instead, strive for his kingdom, and these things will be given to you as well. Do not be afraid, little flock, for it is your Father's good pleasure to give you the kingdom. Sell your possessions, and give alms. Make purses for yourselves that do not wear out, an unfailing treasure in heaven, where no thief comes near and no moth destroys. For where your treasure is, there your heart will be also.

Today is the feast day of Francis, who has been called 'the poor man of Assisi'. Poverty is a key value in Franciscan life, the chosen and joyful poverty of those who trust in God to supply their needs and who make God their treasure.

Francis and Clare both wanted to follow Christ in his poverty. They identified with him as one who had emptied himself of power and become a wanderer, with nowhere to lay his head. This is why Francis was so strict about not having money; in his time, it was a symbol of being rich and secure, and the poor largely lived without it.

But poverty isn't just about money; Francis also wrote about not holding on to reputation, status and even spiritual experience. All of these could also be 'riches' that separated him from following the poor Christ.

The key to joyful poverty is 'do not be afraid' – it is often the fear of going without that makes us play safe and hold on to what we have, and so prevents our generosity. But Jesus invites us to focus on the things of God, in faith that this is the greatest treasure of all. With our hearts fixed on the kingdom, we will be open to receive all the other gifts of God too, gifts that are eternal. And we will be freed to share those gifts with others, confident that we will not be the losers from our generosity.

How might the spirit of Franciscan poverty be expressed in your life and your circumstances?

HELEN JULIAN CSF

Go and make disciples

Now the eleven disciples went to Galilee, to the mountain to which Jesus had directed them. When they saw him, they worshipped him; but some doubted. And Jesus came and said to them, 'All authority in heaven and on earth has been given to me. Go therefore and make disciples of all nations, baptising them in the name of the Father and of the Son and of the Holy Spirit, and teaching them to obey everything that I have commanded you.'

In his *Early Rule*, Francis laid out two means of mission – simple presence and the witness of life; and proclamation. Jesus' command to 'go therefore' was one that Francis and his early brothers took seriously. From 1217 brothers were spreading out into Europe. But Francis longed to go also to places where the gospel had not already been heard.

In 1219, during the Fifth Crusade, Francis reached Damietta on the Nile Delta with some companions. This was very risky; he was beaten by soldiers but eventually reached the Sultan of Egypt and preached to him and his court in word and deed. The Sultan seems to have valued hearing him, and therefore allowed him to preach, but could not convert because of fear of revolt from his people. He offered gifts to Francis, who refused them because of his commitment to poverty, and finally Francis returned in safety to Italy.

Mission can feel difficult enough in our own context; how much more in other lands, among those of other faiths, and in times when faith is often treated as irrelevant at best and dangerous at worst? Francis' model of simple presence, with a willingness to be known as Christian, but 'preaching' only when the moment is right, may seem more possible for many of us. In his encounter with the Sultan, Francis modelled both ways of mission, and has left us a model of interfaith dialogue that is both respectful and risk-taking.

How can the words of Jesus and the example of Francis inspire you to find ways, suited to your life and circumstances, that enable you to carry out the great commission?

HELEN JULIAN CSF

Sunday 6 October — **Luke 10:38–42 (NRSV)**

Seeking balance

Now as they went on their way, [Jesus] entered a certain village, where a woman named Martha welcomed him into her home. She had a sister named Mary, who sat at the Lord's feet and listened to what he was saying. But Martha was distracted by her many tasks; so she came to him and asked, 'Lord, do you not care that my sister has left me to do all the work by myself? Tell her then to help me.' But the Lord answered her, 'Martha, Martha, you are worried and distracted by many things; there is need of only one thing. Mary has chosen the better part, which will not be taken away from her.'

Jesus' years of active ministry were spent very much on the road, but the home of Martha, Mary and Lazarus at Bethany was a place where he could stop for a time, rest and escape the crowds. Martha and Mary are traditionally seen as examples of the active and the contemplative life, respectively, and a balance of these two dimensions was also important to both Francis and Clare.

Francis was mainly on the road, while Clare's life was rooted at San Damiano. There, prayer was the mainspring of the sisters' life, but they also worked within the monastery, both to sustain their own life and to earn money that they could give away. The life of prayer was not one of idleness. And Francis, while spending most of his time travelling, also had times of withdrawal and solitude as an opportunity for deeper and more sustained prayer. Ideally these two dimensions form a virtuous circle in the life of any Christian, with prayer fuelling ministry, and ministry driving us back to prayer. They are like our lungs, which must breathe in and out to sustain our life.

The story of Mary and Martha can seem to downgrade the importance of the active life, but many commentators believe that Jesus is commending Mary for her single-mindedness and her willingness to listen to him, rather than blaming Martha for her practical work.

Who do you most naturally identify with – Mary or Martha? Francis or Clare? How might you bring more of the other dimension into your day-to-day life?

HELEN JULIAN CSF

Monday 7 October   **Galatians 6:14–17 (NRSV)**

Marked by the cross

May I never boast of anything except the cross of our Lord Jesus Christ, by which the world has been crucified to me, and I to the world. For neither circumcision nor uncircumcision is anything; but a new creation is everything! As for those who will follow this rule – peace be upon them, and mercy, and upon the Israel of God. From now on, let no one make trouble for me; for I carry the marks of Jesus branded on my body.

As gifts go, the one that a certain Count Orlando gave Francis in 1213 takes some beating. He gave Francis a mountain – Mount La Verna in Tuscany. From then until the end of his life Francis used it as a place of retreat and prayer.

In August 1224 Francis went there with a few companions, praying alone for 40 days. On 14 September, Holy Cross Day, he set himself to contemplate the passion of Christ and his great love, having asked to feel both the pain of the passion and the love that compelled Christ to suffer so for sinners. In his prayer he had a vision of a six-winged seraph nailed to a cross. Then the marks of the nails and the spear that he'd seen in the seraph began to appear in his own body, and they remained there until his death two years later. These marks are called the stigmata.

Francis was one of the first recorded people to receive the stigmata. Early writers see it as a sign of his deep identification with Christ – his love for Christ made visible in his body. The new life that he was living was expressed in a new gift of God.

It's a daunting example of a Christ-centred life. But perhaps we can start by acknowledging what it is we boast of. Is it what we have achieved or what we have received? If we receive God's gifts of peace and mercy and his forgiveness, and allow them to work in our lives, they will renew us day by day, and move us towards the new creation that is held out to us.

We will not all receive the stigmata, but we are all called to live lives marked by love of God and following of Christ.

HELEN JULIAN CSF

Tuesday 8 October — Mark 10:41–45 (NRSV)

Leading in love

When the ten heard this, they began to be angry with James and John. So Jesus called them and said to them, 'You know that among the Gentiles those whom they recognise as their rulers lord it over them, and their great ones are tyrants over them. But it is not so among you; but whoever wishes to become great among you must be your servant, and whoever wishes to be first among you must be slave of all. For the Son of Man came not to be served but to serve, and to give his life a ransom for many.'

Neither Francis nor Clare set out to found a community or to become a leader. Clare became abbess at San Damiano only reluctantly. She remained abbess until her death, almost 40 years later, but always lived with her sisters, doing the menial tasks, sharing the common dormitory, and writing in her *Rule* that God often revealed what was best to the youngest and newest. Francis resigned as leader of his community of brothers in 1220 and wrote in his *Testament* that he wanted to have a guardian to whom he was responsible, and to obey the minister general. Although the new leaders did not always follow what was important to him, he chose to let go of his power. Even the language he used – guardians, ministers, custodians – speaks of service rather than power.

The paradoxical reversals of which Jesus spoke are seen in the lives of Clare and Francis. Power was not to be used to dominate but to serve. Jesus had set the example by emptying himself of his power and 'taking the form of a slave' (Philippians 2:7). How could his followers not copy him?

Both for leaders and for those led it can be tempting to revert to hierarchical leadership, where the leader makes the decisions and the led carry them out (and can blame the leader if things go wrong). Leadership as service, with consultation, takes more time, and requires more responsibility from everyone. But it is the gospel model, and the one Francis and Clare lived out.

Who is the leader you remember with most affection and respect? What qualities in their leadership could you emulate in your own exercise of servant leadership?

HELEN JULIAN CSF

Wednesday 9 October   **Mark 3:13–19 (NRSV, abridged)**

Drawn in and sent out

[Jesus] went up the mountain and called to him those he wanted, and they came to him. And he appointed twelve, whom he also named apostles, to be with him, and to be sent out to proclaim the message, and to have authority to cast out demons. So he appointed the twelve: Simon… James son of Zebedee and John the brother of James… and Andrew, and Philip, and Bartholomew, and Matthew, and Thomas, and James son of Alphaeus, and Thaddeus, and Simon the Cananaean, and Judas Iscariot, who betrayed him.

'The Lord gave me brothers,' Francis wrote in his *Testament*. He didn't set out to attract men to join him in a new community, but they came anyway. His preaching, which took place not just in churches but also out in the streets, attracted and intrigued them.

Clare's life too attracted women to join her, including several members of her own family and former neighbours. And women in other parts of Italy and beyond were inspired to start their own communities. By the time of her death, 150 communities looked to her for inspiration, as far apart as Prague and Bruges.

Meanwhile Francis' brothers were, like Jesus' disciples, not just called to be with him, but also to be sent out. The first brothers arrived in England in 1224, two years before Francis' death, walking all the way and settling in Canterbury.

This dynamic of being with Jesus and being sent out is crucial to the health of any Christian community. We need to be formed as disciples by sitting at his feet, listening to his teaching and watching him work. But we don't stop there. Like the disciples and the early Franciscans, we are then sent out to share what we have learned. It's easy to want new members to serve the interests of the church or community, to keep the work going, to bring new blood to the rotas. It's harder to attract new people in order to give them away. But that dynamic is part of the reality of discipleship as we see it in the gospel, and in Francis.

Consider any Christian community to which you belong. Does it draw new members to join it? And does it then send them out to do God's work?

HELEN JULIAN CSF

Spirit and life

These twelve Jesus sent out with the following instructions... 'As you go, proclaim the good news, "The kingdom of heaven has come near." Cure the sick, raise the dead, cleanse the lepers, cast out demons. You received without payment; give without payment. Take no gold, or silver, or copper in your belts, no bag for your journey, or two tunics, or sandals, or a staff; for labourers deserve their food. Whatever town or village you enter, find out who in it is worthy, and stay there until you leave.'

This reading inspired Francis. He heard it at Mass on the feast day of Matthias in 1208, and cried out, 'This is what I want; this is what I long for.' And he immediately acted on it, and went on acting on it for the rest of his life. His inspiration was the life of the gospel, and his desire was to imitate the life and ministry of Christ. He and his brothers went out to preach and heal and serve, taking nothing with them, but relying on those they met to feed and accommodate them.

Both Francis and Clare wrote this inspiration into the rules they wrote for their communities. Francis began, 'This is the life of the gospel of Jesus Christ', and Clare wrote that her sisters' form of life is 'to observe the holy gospel of our Lord Jesus Christ'.

Jesus' words make it clear that the apostles were called to a life, not just to a system of belief. And it is a life that is both radical and risky. They set out with only the 'good news', the gospel, to live a life shaped by the imitation of Jesus. And like him they are to depend on those whom they encounter to meet their needs for food and shelter. For most of us, this is probably a risk too far, and we may have genuine responsibilities that prevent us from this radical following. But what risks are we willing to take in our proclamation of the good news?

Both Francis and Clare shaped their lives in imitation of the life of the gospels. What inspires your life of faith? How might the gospels and the life of Christ play a more central part?

HELEN JULIAN CSF

Friday 11 October — Exodus 3:1–5 (NRSV)

Aflame for God

Moses was keeping the flock of his father-in-law Jethro, the priest of Midian; he led his flock beyond the wilderness, and came to Horeb, the mountain of God. There the angel of the Lord appeared to him in a flame of fire out of a bush; he looked, and the bush was blazing, yet it was not consumed. Then Moses said, 'I must turn aside and look at this great sight, and see why the bush is not burned up.' When the Lord saw that he had turned aside to see, God called to him out of the bush, 'Moses, Moses!' And he said, 'Here I am.' Then he said, 'Come no closer! Remove the sandals from your feet, for the place on which you are standing is holy ground.'

Francis and Clare rarely met, but once they shared a meal at St Mary of the Angels with some companions. Francis began to talk about God, and did so with such beauty and sweetness that they forgot the food and, caught up in God's grace, went into a rapture.

The local people saw flames leaping from the chapel and the surrounding forest and rushed to extinguish them. But when they arrived, they found no fire, only Francis and Clare and their companions, aflame in their contemplation of God.

When Clare prayed at San Damiano her sisters often saw a great brilliance above the place where she was, and recalled that she returned from prayer with her face shining and beautiful.

These two stories demonstrate the centrality of prayer to their lives, and the depth of experience to which it took them. Fire is often a sign of God's presence in the Bible, and speaks of the passion and sometimes danger of the human encounter with the divine. Fire can both warm and burn us. Many encounters are, of course, lower-key, but however we come to stand on 'holy ground', it's central to all vocations. Contemplating God, however we go about it, can never be left behind; whatever we do, we also need to spend time simply being in God's presence.

Give me, O God, a greater desire for you. Fill me with your sweet love, and let me shine with your beauty, that the world may see and know you.

HELEN JULIAN CSF

Saturday 12 October   **Philippians 1:3–6, 9–11 (NRSV)**

Keeping the faith

I thank my God every time I remember you, constantly praying with joy in every one of my prayers for all of you, because of your sharing in the gospel from the first day until now. I am confident of this, that the one who began a good work among you will bring it to completion by the day of Jesus Christ… And this is my prayer, that your love may overflow more and more with knowledge and full insight to help you to determine what is best, so that on the day of Christ you may be pure and blameless, having produced the harvest of righteousness that comes through Jesus Christ for the glory and praise of God.

Francis died in 1226, in his mid 40s, but Clare lived until 1253. In those 27 years she had to find her own way, deprived of the guidance and inspiration that had launched her into the life she embraced.

For most of this time she was ill and confined to bed. While Francis burned out quickly and never had to face older age, Clare had to deal with diminishment and weakness. She can perhaps be a model for the older Christian, a saint for the long haul.

Like Paul, Francis and Clare left plenty for others to do. None of them thought they had 'done it all', and they knew that it was God's work that would keep their legacy alive and growing. As Francis lay dying, he said to those around him, 'I have done what was mine to do. May God teach you what is yours to do.' Eight centuries of Franciscans have tried to learn what is theirs to do.

Who do you give thanks to God for in your own journey of faith? Who has nourished and taught and challenged you? Especially if they are no longer with you (or perhaps never were physically – the saints can be great guides), how do you look to God in trust that the work begun through your guides will be brought to completion?

Pray again the prayer at the end of the first day's reading.
What have you learnt from Francis and Clare that might help you
to fulfil God's holy will for your life?

HELEN JULIAN CSF

Introduction

1 Kings 17—22:
The importance of being earnest

Shakespeare wrote, 'All the world's a stage and all the men and women merely players; they have their exits and their entrances, and one man in his time plays many parts' (*As You Like It*, II.vii). The chapters of 1 Kings 17—22 are an unfolding drama; various characters make their entrances and exits, and the director is the Lord, the God of Israel.

Recently studying the downfall of Shakespeare's Macbeth with a student, we noted how ambition, greed and the evil influence of his wife brought him to ruin. I was struck by the similarities to King Ahab. In despair, Macbeth utters the lines, 'Out, out, brief candle! Life's but a walking shadow, a poor player that struts and frets his hour upon the stage and then is heard no more' (V.v). By contrast, the voices of the major and minor characters that we are going to meet in 1 Kings are still heard generation after generation, for their lives were chronicled as part of God's great narrative.

We know that 'all Scripture is God-breathed and is useful for teaching, rebuking, correcting and training in righteousness' (2 Timothy 3:16, NIV). There is an ancient tradition of learning from narrative. Some of my younger students enjoy fables, working out the moral and what the story is 'really all about'. We are going to explore the wisdom that the director is drawing our attention to as we dig below the surface of these Bible narratives, discovering more of what they are 'really all about'.

The characters we will look at are not reciting lines, yet we always find the outcome is in the hands of the director, to whom some characters listen, but others ignore at their peril. Elijah and some of the 'minor' characters show us how to live faith-filled lives in which we stake our all on God's word, moving beyond confessional faith to a deeper dependence on the Lord. We learn that in prayer, we realise and admit our helplessness, and then discover God's provision, power and tenderness. Moreover, these narratives – telling of rejected prophets, miraculous provision, resurrection and the fire of God's presence – foreshadow the second half of God's drama: the coming of Christ and the new covenant.

Curtains up!

FIONA STRATTA

Enter Elijah: going against the flow

Now Elijah, who was from Tishbe in Gilead, told King Ahab, 'As surely as the Lord, the God of Israel, lives – the God I serve – there will be no dew or rain during the next few years until I give the word!' Then the Lord said to Elijah, 'Go to the east and hide by Kerith Brook, near where it enters the Jordan River. Drink from the brook and eat what the ravens bring you, for I have commanded them to bring you food.'

Kerith Brook was in a remote and wild ravine in the Gilead area that Elijah may well have known since his youth. Elijah literally goes against the flow of the brook when he goes into hiding. He has also metaphorically gone against the flow in daring to confront Ahab with God's prophecy that there would be no rain or dew for a few years, until God gave the word through Elijah. Ahab has angered the Lord more than any other king has through his marriage to Jezebel, by building a temple and altar to Baal and joining her in worship, and in encouraging others to worship Baal.

The setting moves to the brook, where God provides Elijah with bread, meat and water. Elijah must have learnt some major life lessons while he was there, preparing him for the challenges ahead. First, he learnt to be humble enough to eat food brought to him miraculously but nevertheless by unclean birds. Next, the supply was sufficient for each meal, brought twice daily – no hoarding was possible. Finally, the brook was gradually drying up, so Elijah had to learn not to fear for the future. There must have been many 'what if' questions arising in his mind that had to be dealt with by the only possible antidote – trust in God.

God often uses one experience or circumstance in our lives to prepare us for the next, shaping our character, increasing our resilience, developing our gifts, preparing us to be in a position to bless others; in short, making us more like Christ.

Reflect on how this has been true in your life and give thanks that 'God causes everything to work together for the good' (Romans 8:28).

FIONA STRATTA

Monday 14 October   **1 Kings 17:13–14 (NLT)**

Enter the widow of Zarephath: acting in faith

But Elijah said to her, 'Don't be afraid! Go ahead and do just what you've said, but make a little bread for me first. Then use what's left to prepare a meal for yourself and your son. For this is what the Lord, the God of Israel, says: There will always be flour and olive oil left in your containers until the time when the Lord sends rain and the crops grow again!'

The brook has dried up, and God has sent Elijah not to a widow in Israel, but to one in Zarephath, near Sidon, from where Queen Jezebel originated, in the heart of a Baal-worshipping land. First ravens, and now a Gentile! The God of Israel is already at work in the widow, for he tells Elijah that he has instructed her to feed him; just how he instructed her we do not know.

The widow, however, is prepared to give him water only, for she and her son are on the brink of starvation. She plans to cook a final meal to eat with her son before they die. Note that the widow does not ask Elijah to join them in this meal; she is struggling to respond to God's instruction, for she knows her own limited resources. But she is to discover that when God calls, he also enables. In this episode he does so through the miraculous supply of olive oil and flour, which feeds the three of them for many days.

We are called both to be wise stewards and to be mindful of others' needs. This can be particularly challenging when we feel near the end of our own resources, whether physical, emotional, mental or financial. In times such as these, we have to be sure of what the Lord is calling us to be and do. There may be times when we, like the widow, can only give to a limited number of people, but for them our gifts can be transformative.

'May the God of peace... equip you with all you need for doing his will. May he produce in you, through the power of Jesus Christ, every good thing that is pleasing to him' (Hebrews 13:20–21).

FIONA STRATTA

Tuesday 15 October   1 Kings 17:21b–24 (NLT)

Enter the widow's son: death and resurrection

[Elijah] cried out to the Lord, 'O Lord my God, please let this child's life return to him.' The Lord heard Elijah's prayer, and the life of the child returned, and he revived! Then Elijah brought him down from the upper room and gave him to his mother. 'Look!' he said. 'Your son is alive!' Then the woman told Elijah, 'Now I know for sure that you are a man of God, and that the Lord truly speaks through you.'

This scene makes uncomfortable reading (although it has a most wonderful conclusion), for the miraculous survival of the three characters is overshadowed by the tragic death of the widow's son. It is uncomfortable to read, because it brings home the reality that obedience to God does not prevent the perplexing mystery of suffering.

    The widow is on a faith journey. Increasingly, she believes that Elijah is a man of God, but she has not yet understood the gracious nature of his God, for she believes that her son's death is a punishment for her sins – a false belief Jesus refutes more than 800 years later (John 9:3). Through the miracle of her son's revival from death, the widow discovers that her fledgling faith is growing to a new maturity, 'now I know for sure' (v. 24). She is blessed with the miracle not only of having her son restored to her, but also of new assurance that the Lord is speaking to her through the prophet.

    In the depths of suffering we too may discover the presence of the Lord in new ways. Like the widow, through our sorrows we may gain spiritual insights and discover more of God's grace. To do so, we need her openness to God and her courage to wrestle with difficult questions. The widow's genuine yet struggling faith is so commendable that Jesus refers to her when he is teaching in Nazareth (Luke 4:25–26). Sadly, through hardened and cynical hearts, the Nazarenes missed experiencing the spiritual life and well-being that Jesus brought elsewhere. They had needed, and so do we, the mustard seed of faith demonstrated by the widow.

Lord, may we understand more of your heart of compassion towards us, full of grace. Soften our hearts. Amen

FIONA STRATTA

Wednesday 16 October   **1 Kings 18:3–4, 7a (NLT)**

Enter Obadiah: two men of courage

So Ahab summoned Obadiah, who was in charge of the palace. (Obadiah was a devoted follower of the Lord. Once when Jezebel had tried to kill all the Lord's prophets, Obadiah had hidden 100 of them in two caves. He put fifty prophets in each cave and supplied them with food and water.)… As Obadiah was walking along, he suddenly saw Elijah coming towards him. Obadiah recognised him at once and bowed down low to the ground before him.

Enter Obadiah, the man holding the highest office in the palace, King Ahab's right-hand man. He is walking on a knife-edge, serving the king and yet maintaining a higher loyalty to God, one that has involved him in risky action.

Now Obadiah faces a further conflict of interest. While searching for water and pasture for the king's horses, he meets Elijah, who is returning on God's instruction. It is the third year of the drought and Elijah is to tell Ahab that God will send rain (1 Kings 18:1–2). The prophet asks Obadiah to tell the king that he is back. Obadiah has shown his submission to God in the way that he greeted Elijah. Nevertheless, Obadiah is convinced that to carry out this command is asking for trouble and will lead to his death. The endless fruitless searches for Elijah in Israel and beyond have infuriated Ahab. Obadiah thinks that by the time he has told the king of Elijah's whereabouts, the Spirit of the Lord will have removed Elijah from danger once again. The king's frustration will be vented on Obadiah for giving him false hope. But he is given Elijah's word, sworn by the Lord Almighty, that the prophet will speak to Ahab that very day. Ahab will come to him – God is setting the agenda. Once again, Obadiah maintains his first loyalty to God and obeys.

Elijah and Obadiah: two courageous men who are wholehearted in their commitment to the Lord, but who have very different 'callings'. Elijah is outside the lion's den and Obadiah is within it. They are both living faithfully in difficult and threatening circumstances.

Lord, may we live faithfully and courageously wherever you have placed us. Grant us wisdom when we find our loyalties are divided. Amen

FIONA STRATTA

Thursday 17 October   **1 Kings 18:18–21 (NLT, abridged)**

Enter Ahab: the Mount Carmel contest

[Elijah said,] 'You and your family are the troublemakers, for you have refused to obey the commands of the Lord and have worshipped the images of Baal instead. Now summon all Israel to join me at Mount Carmel'… So Ahab summoned all the people of Israel and the prophets to Mount Carmel. Then Elijah stood in front of them and said, 'How much longer will you waver, hobbling between two opinions? If the Lord is God, follow him! But if Baal is God, then follow him!' But the people were completely silent.

Ahab goes to meet Elijah and accuses him of being a troublemaker. Those who refuse to go along with the status quo are often labelled in this way. However, Elijah refuses to accept this label and turns the tables on Ahab. Such was Elijah's God-given authority that Ahab agrees to his demand and a huge crowd gathers at Mount Carmel – all Israel, 450 prophets of Baal and 400 of Jezebel's prophets of Asherah. What a moment of opportunity for Elijah! What do you say when such a moment arises? Whatever God's Spirit places on your heart (Matthew 10:19b–20).

In 2018 Bishop Michael Curry was given the opportunity to speak to millions at the royal wedding of Prince Harry and Meghan Markle; he certainly spoke God's word from his heart. Elijah does the same. He tells the people of Israel that they cannot continue with their divided hearts: they must commit themselves totally to following God or Baal. They are about to see the evidence they need to make their choice.

Their unfaithfulness and half-heartedness have prevented them from perceiving God's presence and witnessing his power. In his letter, James cautions us against being double-minded, likening this instability to a wave that is being tossed around by the wind. He warns us that being torn between God and the world hinders us from receiving from the Lord (James 1:6–8).

'Teach me your way, Lord, that I may rely on your faithfulness; give me an undivided heart, that I may fear your name. I will praise you, Lord my God, with all my heart; I will glorify your name forever' (Psalm 86:11–12, NIV).

FIONA STRATTA

Friday 18 October   **1 Kings 18:36–38a (NLT)**

Crowd scene: prayer and fire

At the usual time for offering the evening sacrifice, Elijah the prophet walked up to the altar and prayed, 'O Lord, God of Abraham, Isaac and Jacob, prove today that you are God in Israel and I am your servant. Prove that I have done all this at your command. O Lord, answer me! Answer me so these people will know that you, O Lord, are God and that you have brought them back to yourself.' Immediately the fire of the Lord flashed down from heaven.

First the prophets of Baal call on their god, to no avail. Now it is Elijah's turn. He knows that words will not convince the people, for they have allowed themselves to be swayed by the current majority voice, by state pressure, by the prevalent world view. Only action will demonstrate God's power and authority. Symbolically, Elijah prepares the altar to coincide with the time of the evening sacrifice. The altar is soaked three times with water – a seeming waste of a much-needed resource. Elijah is leaving no room for anyone to claim the fire was a coincidence, resulting from the drought. If the sacrifice catches alight, it will be an undeniable miracle. Perhaps he is also implying by his action that water will soon be plentiful again, so there is no longer a need to limit its usage.

There is a helplessness and vulnerability to Elijah's prayer: he demonstrates utter dependence on God and tremendous faith. If we are honest, we sometimes fear to step out in faith just in case God does not 'come up with the goods'. We can learn much from Elijah's prayers. This one shows his understanding of God's heart, one that lovingly desires to bring his people back to a relationship with him. We also see the motivation behind Elijah's prayer: he longs for the people to know that the Lord is God. His prayers are answered twofold – the fire falls, consuming the sacrifice, and the people return to God in worship.

Perhaps we, too, are living in times when words will not be enough to turn hearts and minds to God; consequently, an outpouring of God's power needs to be earnestly sought after.

FIONA STRATTA

Saturday 19 October   **1 Kings 18:42b–44a (NLT)**

Enter Elijah's servant: witnessing a man in prayer

But Elijah climbed to the top of Mount Carmel and bowed low to the ground and prayed with his face between his knees. Then he said to his servant, 'Go and look out towards the sea.' The servant went and looked, then returned to Elijah and said, 'I didn't see anything.' Seven times Elijah told him to go and look. Finally the seventh time, his servant told him, 'I saw a little cloud about the size of a man's hand rising from the sea.'

Elijah has told Ahab in faith that a mighty rainstorm is coming. Yet there is no sign of it. Ahab turns to celebration and the prophet turns to prayer. His posture in prayer is humble; having just experienced a tremendous act of God, he is now in a spiritual battle. His last prayer was answered powerfully and immediately; this time he has to persevere in prayer. What was the servant learning as he made his seven trips to look out to sea? Eventually, he sees a tiny cloud on the horizon. This is enough to revitalise Elijah, who, on God's strengthening, runs 17 miles to Jezreel.

On occasions we cling to faith when there is little evidence of change. We may be sustained by a few words of encouragement or comfort, or a glimmer of hope indicating change is on its way – the 'little cloud about the size of a man's hand'. This is sufficient to renew our faith and energy, enabling us to continue in our walk (or our run) with the Lord. Sometimes we are aware of divine strengthening as we go through difficult circumstances, empowering us to 'run with purpose in every step' (1 Corinthians 9:26). Other times, when we look back on an experience, we realise the Lord enabled us to persevere. Such perseverance witnesses to those around us.

'The earnest prayer of a righteous person has great power and produces wonderful results. Elijah was as human as we are, and yet when he prayed earnestly that no rain would fall, none fell for three and a half years! Then, when he prayed again, the sky sent down rain and the earth began to yield its crops' (James 5:16b–18).

FIONA STRATTA

Sunday 20 October   **1 Kings 19:1–4a (NLT, abridged)**

Enter Jezebel: Elijah hits rock bottom

When Ahab got home, he told Jezebel everything Elijah had done, including the way he had killed all the prophets of Baal. So Jezebel sent this message to Elijah: 'May the gods strike me and even kill me if by this time tomorrow I have not killed you just as you killed them.' Elijah was afraid and fled for his life… Then he went on alone into the wilderness, travelling all day. He sat down under a solitary broom tree and prayed that he might die.

Elijah goes into hiding again, this time because of Jezebel's reaction to the events at Carmel. He is absolutely devastated by her response; perhaps he had hoped that Ahab and Jezebel would turn to the Lord. If God's proof of power had not changed their hearts and produced in them a desire to lead the people in God's ways, then what would? Elijah's heartache foreshadows the sorrow of our Lord when he grieves over Jerusalem (Matthew 23:37). It is the sorrow known to all who see their ministry rejected.

Perhaps, too, Elijah is burnt out emotionally, spiritually and physically after the exertion of the preceding events. Many who have seen God work in amazing ways may experience fear, disappointment and depression. Elijah escapes to Beersheba, where he leaves his servant and goes on alone into his wilderness experience. Yet he is not alone, for God is there with him, not this time to show his power to the whole nation, but to sustain a much-loved child. There is gentleness about this encounter that contrasts strongly with what has just been. An angel touches Elijah. First his physical and emotional needs are met: time and a place for recuperation – food, drink, sleep, solitude and rest from demanding work.

It can be a shock to find ourselves in a place of exhaustion. Like Elijah, recovering physically, mentally and emotionally takes time and is often a precursor for both a new encounter with God and a new calling.

Lord, thank you for the model you gave us when you instructed your disciples, 'Come with me by yourselves to a quiet place and get some rest' (Mark 6:31, NIV). May we learn to pace ourselves. Amen.

FIONA STRATTA

Monday 21 October — **1 Kings 19:11–13 (NLT)**

Enter the Lord: the sound of a gentle whisper

'Go out and stand before me on the mountain,' the Lord told him. And as Elijah stood there, the Lord passed by, and a mighty windstorm hit the mountain. It was such a terrible blast that the rocks were torn loose, but the Lord was not in the wind. After the wind there was an earthquake, but the Lord was not in the earthquake. And after the earthquake there was a fire, but the Lord was not in the fire. And after the fire there was the sound of a gentle whisper.

In one sense, 'Enter the Lord' is inaccurate, for he is present throughout these narratives – on many occasions we read 'the Lord said'. However, these verses contain an intimate and more prolonged encounter between Elijah and the Lord. The Lord starts by asking Elijah, 'What are you doing here?' (1 Kings 19:9). It is as if he is saying, 'Be honest with me and yourself. What are you thinking and how are you feeling?' Elijah describes his failed ministry (as he sees it), his loneliness and his fear. His perspective is far from God's, yet God tenderly invites Elijah to commune with him in this next stage in the restoration process.

Maybe Elijah expected to experience God in the spectacular – the wind, earthquake and fire. But in this instance, it is in the gentle whisper that Elijah receives God's healing touch. Now he is ready to continue his conversation with the Lord. He does not receive 'answers' to his lament (and nor may we), but he does receive a new assignment: he is to anoint two new kings and a new prophet. God is working out his purposes. His plan for Israel and the wider plan of salvation for the world have not failed. Elijah has been faithful in fulfilling his part, and now he must focus on preparing those who will come after him.

Are there special places where you have known the Lord's touch on your life? Thank God for the times and places where you have received comfort, hope and new direction. Perhaps you sense a need to find space to spend prolonged time with the Lord.

FIONA STRATTA

Tuesday 22 October   **1 Kings 19:19–20 (NLT, abridged)**

Enter Elisha: passing on the baton

So Elijah went and found Elisha son of Shaphat ploughing a field… Elijah went over to him and threw his cloak across his shoulders and then walked away. Elisha left the oxen standing there, ran after Elijah, and said to him, 'First let me go and kiss my father and mother goodbye, and then I will go with you!' Elijah replied, 'Go on back, but think about what I have done to you.'

There are right and wrong reasons for continuing or relinquishing a ministry. We need to be prepared to pass on the baton to someone else at the appropriate time. The instruction to do so has come to Elijah directly from God. For us, it may be the observation of someone's developing gift that we perceive needs the space to grow, or it may be an inner prompting. Elijah has come to the end of one stage in his life and is about to embark on the next: training Elisha. Various emotions may accompany such times: relief, joy, a sense of satisfaction at what has been achieved, or perhaps disappointment, sadness, grief, surprise (even disbelief) that this 'ending' has crept up on us. The most important questions to ask, whatever the limits of our circumstances, are: What do you have for me next, Lord? What is your purpose? Why am I here?

    Elijah recognises the cost of commitment when he instructs Elisha, 'Think about what I have done to you' (v. 20). Elisha's response is unreserved, which must have given Elijah assurance that he was the man for the job. He slaughters his oxen and breaks up his plough – there is to be no turning back, no safety net. Then he celebrates with his family and friends, barbecuing the meat on a fire fuelled by his destroyed plough. Celebration with those we love, alongside a passion for a cause, are God-given treasures that give colour and meaning to our lives. They cannot be bought with money. Elisha already understands wholehearted living and God-centred priorities.

'No one can serve two masters. For you will hate one and love the other; you will be devoted to one and despise the other. You cannot serve God and be enslaved to money' (Matthew 6:24).

FIONA STRATTA

Wednesday 23 October   **1 Kings 20:23, 25, 28 (NLT, abridged)**

Enter Ben-hadad: limiting God

After their defeat, Ben-hadad's officers said to him, 'The Israelite gods are gods of the hills; that is why they won. But we can beat them easily on the plains… Recruit another army like the one you lost'… So King Ben-hadad did as they suggested… Then the man of God went to the king of Israel and said, 'This is what the Lord says:… I will defeat this vast army for you. Then you will know that I am the Lord.'

King Ben-hadad of Aram has besieged Israel's capital, Samaria, and threatened total destruction. Ahab taunts him, 'A warrior putting on his sword for battle should not boast like a warrior who has already won' (1 Kings 20:11). These words inflame Ben-hadad's anger, and he plans an attack on Samaria. However, a prophet passes on the Lord's instructions to King Ahab as to how they can win the battle. Ahab listens and victory is theirs. The prophet predicts that Ben-hadad will attack again in the spring.

Ben-hadad makes the mistake of believing that his strength and power will bring success. His officers advise him that the Israelites can succeed only in the hill country and not on the plains, where different fighting skills are needed. Thus Ben-hadad believes that there are limits to the God of Israel's power. However, the Israelites are to experience a great victory that, reminiscent of Jericho, involves the collapse of walls. God has brought down walls before and once again his intervention frees his people from their enemies. But God desires to do more than this: he yearns for Ahab to know that he is the Lord and to recognise God's hand in their success.

We can consciously or subconsciously limit what we believe God can do. He longs to break down strongholds in our lives in order to bring us into greater inner freedom. We battle 'not by force nor by strength, but by my Spirit, says the Lord of Heaven's Armies' (Zechariah 4:6).

Lord, may we turn to you for 'divine power to demolish strongholds' (2 Corinthians 10:4, NIV), that we may know you and walk closely with you in humble recognition of your hand in our lives. Amen

FIONA STRATTA

Thursday 24 October **1 Kings 21:1–3 (NLT, abridged)**

Enter Naboth: ultimate authority

Now there was a man named Naboth, from Jezreel, who owned a vineyard in Jezreel beside the palace of King Ahab of Samaria. One day Ahab said to Naboth, 'Since your vineyard is so convenient to my palace, I would like to buy it to use as a vegetable garden…' But Naboth replied, 'The Lord forbid that I should give you the inheritance that was passed down by my ancestors.'

Ahab's plans to take Naboth's vineyard are thwarted and, rather than admiring Naboth's honourable response, he becomes angry and resentful. Ahab lets himself come under Jezebel's influence, and her treachery gives him what he thought would bring him happiness – a patch of land.

It takes a brave man to stand up against a powerful one who had decided to use his dominant position for personal gain. It costs Naboth his life. Such courage continues to cost people their lives. We are called to pray that those in power will use their position for the common good, for God's will to be done through them 'on earth, as it is in heaven' (Matthew 6:10). We also need to pray for and seek ways to support those who take a costly stand against corruption, that they will be delivered from evil (Matthew 6:13).

Like Naboth, Elijah is prepared to resist evil. On God's command, he confronts Ahab. Elijah knows the God who is above all earthly authority and therefore ultimately has greater power than the king. This knowledge has permeated his being to such an extent that he has the courage to speak out against injustice. Elijah's life is spared; Naboth's is taken from him. This and many other situations are beyond our comprehension. Yet in a world full of injustice, God's final justice gives us hope and courage.

'Understand the incredible greatness of God's power for us who believe him. This is the same mighty power that raised Christ from the dead and seated him in the place of honour at God's right hand in the heavenly realms. Now he is far above any ruler or authority or power or leader or anything else – not only in this world but also in the world to come'
(Ephesians 1:19a–21).

FIONA STRATTA

Friday 25 October   **1 Kings 22:17, 26a, 28 (NLT)**

Enter Micaiah: true prophet

Then Micaiah told [Ahab], 'In a vision I saw all Israel scattered on the mountains, like sheep without a shepherd. And the Lord said, "Their master has been killed. Send them home in peace"'… 'Arrest him!' the king of Israel ordered… But Micaiah replied, 'If you return safely, it will mean that the Lord has not spoken through me!' Then he added to those standing around, 'Everyone mark my words!'

Elijah has foretold the destruction of Ahab's family. Ahab reacts to God's word with repentance, and God responds by showing mercy and postponing judgement (1 Kings 21:29). Perhaps at times we feel uncomfortable with God's longing to be merciful to those who openly flaunt his ways. We do not know how Elijah responds, but we do know that three years of peace follow.

However, Ahab's remorse fades and he plans an attack on the king of Aram. Four hundred of Ahab's prophets foresee the Lord's granting success. Ahab is reluctant to hear what the prophet Micaiah has to say, for he believes Micaiah prophesies only doom and gloom. Sure enough, Micaiah foresees defeat and Ahab's death. Maybe, like Ahab, there are times when we want to hear the truth only if it is positive. We all need relationships in which we feel safe enough to be challenged, the aim being to grow and mature in Christ. In such encounters though, we need to 'speak the truth in love' (Ephesians 4:15) and remember the call to gentleness.

Micaiah refuses to be a king-pleaser, and the price he pays is imprisonment. He declares that the outcome of the battle will speak for itself, for the truth of a prophecy shows itself in its fulfilment. Four hundred prophets foresee success, and one foresees defeat. The majority voice is not necessarily the correct one. In an age of political correctness, it can be a tough challenge to go against the flow, ignoring the status quo. Micaiah insists, 'I will say only what the Lord tells me to say' (1 Kings 22:14). We can learn from his example and refuse to people-please.

Lord, may we, like Micaiah, speak with honesty and frankness when appropriate opportunities arise. May we do so with humility, courage, clarity, gentleness and love. Amen

FIONA STRATTA

Saturday 26 October   **1 Kings 22:29–30a, 34a, 37a (NLT)**

Enter an Aramean soldier

So King Ahab of Israel and King Jehoshaphat of Judah led their armies against Ramoth-gilead. The king of Israel said to Jehoshaphat, 'As we go into battle, I will disguise myself so no one will recognise me, but you wear your royal robes'… An Aramean soldier, however, randomly shot an arrow at the Israelite troops and hit the king of Israel between the joints of his armour… So the king died.

The battle is about to commence and Ahab has a plan to survive. Ahab disguises himself as an ordinary soldier, hiding himself among his men. However, an arrow from an unnamed soldier somehow hits Ahab in the gap between parts of his armour. There was nowhere that Ahab could hide from the Lord; no amount of encircling soldiers could prevent the destination of the randomly shot arrow. The Lord has longed to lead Ahab in the paths of righteousness and justice through the words of his prophets. He has demonstrated his loving-kindness and mercy, but Ahab has rejected this. Now, in the final scene of Ahab's life, we see the outworking of the proverb, 'Many are the plans in a person's heart, but it is the Lord's purpose that prevails' (Proverbs 19:21, NIV).

Ahab watches the battle from the sidelines until sunset, when he dies. His life has been a tragedy of poor decisions and wasted opportunities, giving a disastrous example to his son, Ahaziah, who repeats his father's mistakes in his two-year reign and further angers the Lord.

The dramatic demise of Ahab shows us that God does and will always have the final say. We rejoice in knowing that God is a God of judgement, as well as of love, when throughout the world we see the havoc and suffering caused by evil leaders and regimes.

For those who love and follow the Lord, it is a comfort to know that there is nowhere we can hide from him. For in him we have shelter, a refuge and a fortress. Our lives, whether short or long, are 'hidden with Christ in God' (Colossians 3:3).

Lord, 'I can never escape from your Spirit! I can never get away from your presence!' (Psalm 139:7). Thank you! Amen

FIONA STRATTA

Introduction

Exile (Part 2)

Some events in life are seminal. Everything that happens from that moment onwards is deeply affected by the event, whether for good or for ill. So it was when the people of God were transported (and then trafficked, we might say) from their homeland to Babylon in the sixth century BC. This was not the first time the Hebrews had been exiled, but it was by far the most devastating of such events, shattering their view of God, their idea of promise, their identity and their future hopes. And yet from this devastation came a new experience and a new understanding of God that surpassed the faith they had once possessed.

Those who had foreseen the outcome of faithless living also pointed to a time when the Lord God would re-establish blessing and harmony to the land and people. The Hebrews would never forget what had taken place but would discover God differently, understanding their history, story and Saviour in a new way. This would be utterly transformative and shape expectations about the coming Messiah.

In these readings we will see how the exile continued to shape faith in the New Testament. On occasions this experience was literal, as when John found himself on Patmos or when Peter reminded the faithful that, though dispersed and apart from their Lord, they were nonetheless part of the church and fellow citizens with all God's people. On other occasions we see how exile provided a lens, a metaphor which helped interpret the redemptive work of the Lord Jesus. We will encounter those who were exiled from every human engagement but found in Jesus their true homecoming and place of refuge.

What we will also see is that God is not absent from these events, but that the journey through what can be a dark night of the soul has the capacity to deepen faith and trust in God. When we stand on the other side of the exile, we exercise new eyes of faith and find hope deepened by our experiences.

I hope and pray that you discover the God of restoring grace each day and find faith renewed and hope rekindled.

ANDY JOHN

Sunday 27 October — Isaiah 5:13–14 (NIV)

Losing my religion

Therefore my people will go into exile for lack of understanding; those of high rank will die of hunger and the common people will be parched with thirst. Therefore Death expands its jaws, opening wide its mouth; into it will descend their nobles and masses with all their brawlers and revellers.

Sometime in the eighth century BC, the Assyrian army attacked the northern kingdom of Israel and, after sacking the capital, Samaria, deported thousands to their homeland as slaves and exiles. We cannot be certain how many were taken, but the number would have been in the tens of thousands and the effect on the kingdom devastating. Unlike the more significant deportation of the southern kingdom in the sixth century, which was ended when King Cyrus issued a decree allowing for their return, there was no restoration for the northern tribes.

The act of stealing human beings is the one of the most psychologically destructive. It robs us of identity, community, economy and personal freedom. Witness the harrowed faces on young girls abducted by Boko Haram. Should something similar happen again today it would hold the attention of our news media for months.

And yet this destruction did not happen without warning. Prophets such as Amos and Hosea had seen that national life was desperate. Amos even wrote his prophecy of doom to a funeral dirge to mark the death of the nation (Amos 5). For the first time in their history, the prophets called the whole nation to account for the rot that had set in.

The significance of Israel's experience is not hard to see. We need truth-telling more than ever in an age when so-called fake news abounds. We need prophets to reimagine and retell what flourishing, connected and godly communities look like. Living and telling lives of goodness and grace is not for the few but for us all. Exile or not, the well-being of a land lies in its people.

Lord God, you inspire new messengers of truth in every age. Make your ways known upon earth so we may see the ways and walk in them. Amen

ANDY JOHN

Monday 28 October — Jeremiah 13:19–21 (NIV)

Deportation to Babylon

The cities in the Negev will be shut up, and there will be no one to open them. All Judah will be carried into exile, carried completely away. Look up and see those who are coming from the north. Where is the flock that was entrusted to you, the sheep of which you boasted? What will you say when the Lord sets over you those you cultivated as your special allies? Will not pain grip you like that of a woman in labour?

When the Babylonian empire attacked Jerusalem in 597BC, much of the population was carried into exile. An attempt to overthrow foreign rule later resulted in the destruction of the walls and temple. As the Assyrians had plundered Israel, so now the Babylonians exiled the southern kingdom of Judah and appeared to bring the nation to an end.

This second deportation was probably larger than the first. It was also more profoundly felt than the first and is probably, alongside the exodus, the event that most shaped faith in the Hebrews for the next 500 years. Why was this?

This new exile caused a crisis of identity. A people living on land given by promise understand their identity as being bound up with the place where they live. With the loss of land and all that goes with it, something of the people's soul was lost.

Second, there was a crisis of faith. The land and oversight of God in covenant were all part of the one promise. Had God changed, forgotten his oath or, worse, in his anger had had enough and washed his hands of the rebellious nation, as he did of the people in Noah's day?

These terrible events were painful for the people of God. And yet from the ashes of despair something new developed in the experience of the exiles: they began to hope. And hope is the beginning of change. It is the means by which we see a new future and what is needed to deliver it.

Lord, it isn't easy to find hope sometimes. We can feel abandoned. Give us patience at times like this so that hope, in your Son, can grow within us. Amen

ANDY JOHN

Tuesday 29 October   **Psalm 137:1–4 (NIV)**

We lay down and wept

By the rivers of Babylon we sat and wept when we remembered Zion. There on the poplars we hung our harps, for there our captors asked us for songs, our tormentors demanded songs of joy; they said, 'Sing us one of the songs of Zion!' How can we sing the songs of the Lord while in a foreign land?

You will probably know of the music group Boney M for one song above all others: 'Rivers of Babylon'. The psalm from which the song is written is, however, less inviting than a pop song. In fact, it's a lament, a song of despair, which issues in a final outburst of uncontrolled anger and rage. This is one of the songs of the exiles.

    Recall that the Judeans have been deported to a new land by the Babylonians. Here they struggle to retain their identity and way of life, so much of which was bound up with what Abraham had been promised by God (Genesis 17). And those who rule over them now seek some sport – a song to cheer them. We can imagine the reason for this: not only to brighten their day but to re-enforce the cruel reality that the Judeans are a conquered people. The request for a song is a taunt.

    We might have all felt something similar to this: the loss of a loved one, employment or a friendship that cuts the very ground from beneath us, and we flounder without the security we have taken for granted for so long. We too feel conquered. It is bewildering, disorientating and painful.

    Discovering life beyond the loss of our former securities might take time and patient waiting, and we will need space and support. God knows this and gives it. In the period of acclimatising to our situation, we will need to remember that this period is not forever nor is it the end. God always journeys with us towards the light of his presence. Take this with you today.

Gracious God, when I feel like raging or despairing, speak words deep into my soul. I want to discover you afresh today. In Jesus' name.

ANDY JOHN

Wednesday 30 October — Lamentations 5:19–22 (NIV)

Abandoned and forgotten

You, Lord, reign forever; your throne endures from generation to generation. Why do you always forget us? Why do you forsake us so long? Restore us to yourself, Lord, that we may return; renew our days as of old unless you have utterly rejected us and are angry with us beyond measure.

We have seen that the exile created a crisis that had many layers. Apart from the suffering of deportation and land loss, the Hebrews began to wonder if and fear that God, too, had abandoned them. No one explores this possibility more than the writer of Lamentations.

We are familiar with his thoughts but often fast forward to that glorious passage beginning: 'The steadfast love of the Lord never ceases, his mercies never come to an end; they are new every morning; great is your faithfulness' (Lamentations 3:22–23, NRSV). We dwell less on the 'wormwood and gall' (3:19, NRSV) and the tears that flow unceasingly at the destruction of the beloved nation (3:48). We do not like to live with the tantalising, painful thought of utter rejection. The writer himself never resolves this tension, fearing the worst and hoping for the best.

It is not hard to see why this crisis arose. The promise of a covenant rested on God's word to Abraham and was for all ages (Genesis 15:1–6). It was not only a promise of land but also of God's continuing presence. In exile, it seemed that with the loss of land, God too had departed.

Many of us might have played with this same thought. We might have felt we had sinned so badly that God had finally cut us off and no amount of pleading would change his mind. It might be that life has been difficult and we cannot experience God in the midst of pain or confusion. We feel like the exiles.

We should note that even here the writer is still talking to God, still searching. His crisis is the very thing he brings to God. The seeds of hope lie in this longing, crying and searching, because God will not always be silent. Today, hold to this and bring your cries to God.

God of infinite goodness, in the midst of dark times, stay with me so that I may find you whom to know is life itself. Amen

ANDY JOHN

Thursday 31 October   **Jeremiah 4:9–10 (NIV)**

Forsaken

'In that day,' declares the Lord, 'the king and the officials will lose heart, the priests will be horrified, and the prophets will be appalled.' Then I said, 'Alas, Sovereign Lord! How completely you have deceived this people and Jerusalem by saying, "You will have peace," when the sword is at our throats!'

The exile created various crises in the life of God's people: they believed that the land, theirs by promise, was lost; they believed that God had abandoned them; and, in today's text, their very existence as a people seems threatened.

The prophet Jeremiah was among those who had warned that faithlessness would have catastrophic consequences (Jeremiah 20:6), and he urged repentance because God might yet be merciful (14:7). However, he also urged an acceptance of the exile, because this was God's will, and attacked those who prophesied a quick end to the Babylonian onslaught (28:15).

The loss of a nation's identity, its faith and future, is devastating, but what is imagined in these words brings us to the brink of despair. Here, it is the annihilation of the nation which Jeremiah contemplates. He prays for a fountain of tears with which to lament for the slain of his people (9:1). When our very existence is threatened and we can only stare at the darkness, it can appear that everything is lost. Those who have suffered in wars or from some other personal trauma or who face a future that is deeply etched with suffering and loss know this experience. It is not dissimilar to the cry of Jesus from the cross: 'My God, my God, why have you forsaken me?' (Matthew 27:46).

Sometimes it is only the faith of others that holds us at such times or when we look back and find God in the background, nearer to us than we had thought. Then the darkness is pierced with a new light and hope breaks upon us.

Lord, we need faith that sees in the darkness and leads to better places. Walk with us each step of the way, we pray. In Jesus' name.

ANDY JOHN

Friday 1 November — Ezekiel 1:1–3 (NIV)

Rediscovering God in a strange land

In my thirtieth year, in the fourth month on the fifth day, while I was among the exiles by the River Kebar, the heavens were opened and I saw visions of God. On the fifth of the month – it was the fifth year of the exile of King Jehoiachin – the word of the Lord came to Ezekiel the priest, the son of Buzi, by the River Kebar in the land of the Babylonians. There the hand of the Lord was on him.

When in exile and when all seemed hopeless, something unexpected happened in the life of God's people. They met with God in the 'foreign land' (Psalm 137:4). Our verses for today read simply, but their significance cannot be overstated: when the prophet Ezekiel, an exile, encountered God in Babylon, this event shattered the notion that the God of Judah was to be found only in the land of Judah.

This encounter was groundbreaking in the way it opened new doors of hope that exile and the absence of God might not be the end. There are two things we might understand here. First, God was not land-limited in the way they had supposed. Into the crises, God spoke with new energy and urgency. This completely changed the way the Hebrews understood God. Second, there came a new mandate: the exiles were called to new life as God granted them a new spirit and a new heart (Ezekiel 11:19). If the Hebrews had failed to live to the standards set under the first covenant, God would give them all they needed to be faithful in the future. This revelation prepared the way for their return and has significance for the message of the New Testament.

But for us too in our immediate situations it is profoundly important. God will not be boxed in by human failing and will surprise us with acts of new mercy for which we may be totally unprepared.

Lord, you never fail to surprise us with the mystery of your ways. Break into our lives afresh, give us new heart and voice and lead us forward in Jesus' name. Amen

ANDY JOHN

All Saint's Day

Saturday 2 November   **Isaiah 52:7–9 (NIV)**

Beautiful on the mountains

How beautiful on the mountains are the feet of those who bring good news, who proclaim peace, who bring good tidings, who proclaim salvation, who say to Zion, 'Your God reigns!' Listen! Your watchmen lift up their voices; together they shout for joy. When the Lord returns to Zion, they will see it with their own eyes. Burst into songs of joy together, you ruins of Jerusalem, for the Lord has comforted his people, he has redeemed Jerusalem.

When Cyrus, the Persian king, decreed that the Hebrews were free to return to their homeland, it was not only unexpected but transforming. In Ezekiel, God was presented as the shepherd searching for the sheep to bring them home (Ezekiel 34:11). In Jeremiah, God was the tender parent safeguarding the new family (Jeremiah 31:1, 20). And in our verses today, it is God the great victor who goes ahead of the exiles to prepare the way for a new future.

As God had taken his people from their land, so it was God who now restored their fortunes and turned mourning into joyful dancing. This unexpected grace is described as the sovereign power of God, who shapes history and commands even the foreign emperors to do his bidding.

Our verses today complete one part of the story. But it would be a mistake to think that this was simply a return to what had been the status quo prior to the exile. God's people are indeed restored, but they understand their story, their faith and their God differently. Something deep in their soul has shifted.

My own experience of dark times is at one with this. When the clouds part and God shines light into our situations, something changes within us and our faith is made stronger; our vision of God is expanded. I have found this to be true even in suffering. It is never easy when we are in the midst of dark times, our own 'exile', but somehow a new thing, a new joyful faith, can emerge as a consequence.

Lord, call me towards the light of your presence so that I may walk in freedom and faithfulness in you. Amen

ANDY JOHN

Sunday 3 November — Matthew 1:12–16 (NIV)

Jesus, the new homeland

After the exile to Babylon: Jeconiah was the father of Shealtiel, Shealtiel the father of Zerubbabel, Zerubbabel the father of Abihud, Abihud the father of Eliakim, Eliakim the father of Azor, Azor the father of Zadok, Zadok the father of Akim, Akim the father of Elihud, Elihud the father of Eleazar, Eleazar the father of Matthan, Matthan the father of Jacob, and Jacob the father of Joseph, the husband of Mary, and Mary was the mother of Jesus who is called the Messiah.

I have yet to preach on the genealogies in scripture, but our verse today would be a good place to start. We also mark a move to the New Testament and will discover how powerfully the writers wield the theme of exile as they describe the significance of Jesus. We will see how 'exile', developed in the Old Testament, is recrafted in the New and explore its layers in the days ahead.

This list is important because it verifies lines of blood from the deposed Jeconiah to the birth of the Messiah. Matthew continues his ordered description beyond the genealogy (Matthew 1:17) to show how carefully history is shaped by God. We have not arrived at this point by accident. But of greater importance still is the fact that a messiah is mentioned at all.

Tracing the exile in the Old Testament allowed us to see a restored people inhabiting their homeland in renewed obedience to God. But the reality of this hope depended on fidelity within the community of faith. With hindsight, we see how limited were the boundaries of peace. When Jesus was born, the land was again occupied.

Matthew's subtle insertion of the word 'Messiah' is vital because we are invited to understand that exile is something more than physical and that the people are still in bondage. Their real freedom will not be secured by an exit of the occupying forces but by something quite different. It is the Messiah, the anointed and true king, who will set his people free.

Lord Jesus, Messiah, born to set us free, come and reign in us who mourn in lonely exile here. For your name's sake.

ANDY JOHN

Monday 4 November **Acts 2:5–8 (NIV)**

Homecoming

Now there were staying in Jerusalem God-fearing Jews from every nation under heaven. When they heard this sound, a crowd came together in bewilderment, because each one heard their own language being spoken. Utterly amazed, they asked: 'Aren't all these who are speaking Galileans? Then how is it that each of us hears them in our native language?'

When Luke records the coming of the Holy Spirit on the disciples, he knows his message is no less explosive than the wind and fire that accompanied the occasion. The gift of the Holy Spirit was a sign that the end times had arrived (Acts 2:17), that God's enduring presence would not be limited to the great and the good. With the advent of God's kingdom in Jesus, God was doing something new in his world.

The crowds, themselves from diverse backgrounds, all witness the spectacle of God's praises ringing out – all in different languages but sharing one essential message; they witness the new era of God's kingdom. So, what does this passage actually mean?

We are seeing that the promise of the Messiah would herald a different kind of freedom for God's people, which transcended geography and invited deeper transformation. The church's 'birthday' at Pentecost marks this moment: the disciples are given a new language of praise, because they are enjoying a new relationship with God. Exiles were unable to sing the Lord's song in a strange land (Psalm 137:4); here they spill over in adoration. If once they were apart from Zion, outside the sphere of God's blessing, here they encounter the very presence of God, demonstrated by the fire, as in the time of Moses (Exodus 3:2), and wind like a violent storm (Psalm 18:10).

This new reality put in place the way God would bless all people in the future. It is by God's Spirit that we are fully immersed in the life of God and no longer excluded or on the sidelines. Rejoice today that you are among good company and blessed by God.

Father, thank you for the gift of your Spirit, who draws us deeper into the life of your Son Jesus. May I go that way faithfully in his name. Amen

ANDY JOHN

Tuesday 5 November   Mark 5:14–16 (NIV)

Ransomed, healed, restored, forgiven

Those tending the pigs ran off and reported this in the town and countryside, and the people went out to see what had happened. When they came to Jesus, they saw the man who had been possessed by the legion of demons, sitting there, dressed and in his right mind; and they were afraid. Those who had seen it told the people what had happened to the demon-possessed man – and told about the pigs as well.

In this most dramatic of stories, we encounter a man, utterly lost and helpless, an exile in every sense, who is wonderfully restored and brought home. The story of the Gadarene demoniac pits the power of Jesus to save and heal, even with sharp, demanding consequences for others, against the narrow self-interests of those affected by the miracle.

In our readings, we are seeing that the restoration of God's people from their bondage and slavery, a key theme of the exile, is much more than a matter of geography, land or economy. There is a deeper slavery than that of the human chain (however dreadful that is) from which we need liberating. This possessed man was excluded from every conceivable dignity and opportunity. He was an outcast from the religious community, despised by peers, penniless and abandoned, perhaps even driven, to the local graveyard. In the words of Paul, he was 'without hope and without God in the world' (Ephesians 2:12).

His world changed dramatically when he encountered Jesus. Literally, and not just figuratively, his chains fell off and he was free and 'in his right mind' (v. 15). When we encounter God reaching out and into the very core of our soul, it is a profound moment. It is the occasion when darkness is dispelled, and we are invited to walk into the light of his love. It is at this point we know our true homecoming and that whatever kind of exile we may have experienced, Christ has set us free and brought us home.

Lord Jesus Christ, you set the prisoners free to new life and hope. Lead us from darkness to light that we may walk with you closely each day. Amen

ANDY JOHN

Wednesday 6 November   **Galatians 3:26–29 (NIV)**

In Christ

So in Christ Jesus you are all children of God through faith, for all of you who were baptised into Christ have clothed yourselves with Christ. There is neither Jew nor Gentile, neither slave nor free, nor is there male and female, for you are all one in Christ Jesus. If you belong to Christ, then you are Abraham's seed, and heirs according to the promise.

We saw in our earlier readings that one of the most desperate aspects of exile in the Old Testament was the loss of identity. This happened when the story of faith threatened to disappear and when, surrounded by a culture that was hostile, the people of God began to lose connection with their roots and their history. With this diminution, they lost cohesion and the sense that they were different from the nations around them with a unique call to belong to God. After he had attended to the walls of Jerusalem, Nehemiah quickly attended to the restoration of communal life and re-established patterns to support faithfulness to God (Nehemiah 13). He realised that the identity of the Hebrews had been lost.

Paul's contention in these verses is that something fundamental happens when we believe in Jesus. To belong to him (be 'baptised') is to be clothed with him in a way that links his identity with our own. And this association of grace happens to all, whether we are slave or free, male or female. For Paul, this belonging is the new creation (2 Corinthians 5:17) that God brings into being. This is not merely a piece of sociology, indicating the inclusiveness of God's offer, but establishes the new identity of the people of God.

If the exile occasioned the stripping of personality and identity, faith in Christ brings a new name and a new identity that are ours for all time. It might be poetic licence, but it is not far from the truth when we say our names are written on the palm of his hand.

Lord Jesus Christ, you have given me a new name and status as your friend and brother. Teach me to live in the truth and light of this new grace. Amen

ANDY JOHN

Thursday 7 November   **1 Peter 2:10–12 (NIV)**

True to God

Once you were not a people, but now you are the people of God; once you had not received mercy, but now you have received mercy. Dear friends, I urge you, as foreigners and exiles, to abstain from sinful desires, which wage war against your soul. Live such good lives among the pagans that, though they accuse you of doing wrong, they may see your good deeds and glorify God on the day he visits us.

Peter is one of the few New Testament writers who uses specifically the word 'exile', even if the idea lies deep in the thinking of others. This verse makes sense only once we realise he is writing to the dispersed believers in the Middle East (1 Peter 1:1); that is, to those who are far from Jerusalem, the heart of the Christian faith.

But Peter's use of the word cannot refer only to a physical separation from Jerusalem, because he links it to faithfulness to God. 'Exiles' are in danger of losing the battle against sin because the threat is that they lose connection with the whole body of Christ and their Lord. Peter's underlying supposition is that separation from a living faith community makes walking closely with God that much more challenging.

I recall a sermon many years ago when the preacher spoke of the coals that fall from the fire: how quickly they lose their heat, whereas in the blaze of the hearth, they provide all the warmth and glow needed. So our verse is a stark and direct challenge to go-it-alone Christianity and the attitude that says, 'I do not need the church.' The church may well be full of sinful people, but it is also the place where we are nurtured and where we learn. To belong fully to this even dispersed gathering of disciples is to be true to God and to walk forwards with confidence.

Father, we need good support from others and a place where we can give too. Help us in our churches, even when we find it hard, to see them as spaces in which we can grow closer to you and others. Amen

ANDY JOHN

Friday 8 November   **Revelation 1: 9–11 (NIV)**

Patmos and wisdom

I, John, your brother and companion in the suffering and kingdom and patient endurance that are ours in Jesus, was on the island of Patmos because of the word of God and the testimony of Jesus. On the Lord's Day I was in the Spirit, and I heard behind me a loud voice like a trumpet, which said: 'Write on a scroll what you see and send it to the seven churches: to Ephesus, Smyrna, Pergamum, Thyatira, Sardis, Philadelphia and Laodicea.'

Throughout our readings we have seen how exile is both a physical reality in the Old Testament and a spiritual reality in the New. The promise of restoration envisaged a new period of grace for God's people. A new covenant would be inaugurated, and the people would have new hearts with which to love God more truly: 'I will remove the heart of stone from their flesh and give them a heart of flesh' (Ezekiel 11:19b, NRSV). If Jesus was God's ultimate 'restoration', whose presence brought near the kingdom of God, we can see how this dynamic worked in the life of those who were imprisoned and set free (Mark 5:15).

However, John's experience on Patmos, literally exiled, flows in a different direction and opens new perspectives on how God uses isolation and hardship as the way of bringing blessing. Reading this short passage connects us closely with the way Ezekiel met God in exile. Then it was something altogether new for the Lord to address people in a foreign land. John experienced not only the immediacy of God's address but also the command to listen and record words for the churches of Asia Minor.

I think these are connected. Although this isolation must have been hugely challenging for John, it was here that he heard from God. When there is space for God, even when it is imposed space, we can claim it for God. I think again of those who live with enforced space and face different challenges. God is not far from us. The exile of our present time can become a place of deep encounter.

God of all opportunity, draw near in times when I am isolated and when I am not. Become my all in all, in Jesus' name.

ANDY JOHN

Saturday 9 November — Revelation 22:1–3a (NIV)

A new homeland

Then the angel showed me the river of the water of life, as clear as crystal, flowing from the throne of God and of the Lamb down the middle of the great street of the city. On each side of the river stood the tree of life, bearing twelve crops of fruit, yielding its fruit every month. And the leaves of the tree are for the healing of the nations. No longer will there be any curse.

Our final reading brings us full circle and is a fitting end to our exploration of exile. Again, in a way reminiscent of Old Testament prophets, John combines a strong visual and physical description of the new Jerusalem (beginning at Revelation 21) with the deep spiritual layers found in the pages of the New Testament.

The reading weaves together imagery from the Old Testament but locates it all in the final saving work of God and the Lamb. In other words, here we see our final resting place, our true home where the reign of God is unfettered by human sin and a broken creation. Apart from our Lord, we might say we remain in a kind of exile in the way that great Advent carol describes ('O Come, O Come Emmanuel'). We are never truly 'home' until we are with Christ in full and unbroken communion.

This vision of a good end for the people of God was clearly written as a hopeful sign that God would never be defeated. It announced that, whether God's people are literally in exile (as was John on Patmos) or facing some other form of isolation and hardship, the sovereign God would have the victory.

This is the message we can take with us from this series: whatever our circumstances, however bleak they may seem, God has always rescued the exiles. Even when all seems lost, there is a space to find God anew and differently. I hope and pray you will find God like this and that your faith will be strengthened.

Lord, you bring us out of darkness. Help us to walk in the light now and for all time with you.

ANDY JOHN

Introduction

Psalm 119

In the beginning was the Word…

The first thing that strikes one about Psalm 119 is its length. With 176 verses it is the longest psalm; indeed, it is the longest chapter in the Bible and longer than 31 of the books of the Bible. It's long!

Then consider its highly elaborate structure. It has 22 sections of eight verses, each beginning with a different letter of the Hebrew alphabet: it is an acrostic. The whole psalm is a carefully created labour of love. That becomes even more apparent when you begin reading it. Nearly every verse includes one of eight synonyms for the word of God – variously translated (in the NIV) as: law, commands, decrees, word, laws, precepts, statutes and promise.

'But wait,' you cry, 'This sounds awfully legalistic. Haven't we left all those rules and regulations behind?'

Notice two things. First, the most frequent of these eight words is *tora*. This is also the name given to the first five books of the Bible, which contain much more than laws. Indeed, the root verb for *tora* means 'to teach'. So this word alone hints at the full teaching of the scriptures, the revelation of God.

Second, Psalm 119 is not focused on rules and regulations. It is focused on God. Nearly every verse is addressed to God, and refers to 'your law, your statutes, your decrees'.

Richard Wurmbrand was a Romanian pastor imprisoned for 14 years, and the author of *Tortured for Christ* (1966). When asked, 'Which Bible verse helped and strengthened you in those circumstances?', he answered, '*No* Bible verse was of any help… it was never meant by God that Psalm 23 should strengthen you. It is the Lord who can strengthen you. It is not enough to have the psalm. You must have the one about whom the psalm speaks.'

Genesis 1 reveals that God spoke the whole of creation into reality: 'And God said' (NIV). John 1 begins, 'In the beginning was the Word, and the Word was with God, and the Word was God' (NIV). Psalm 119 is a uniquely crafted celebration of the God who is revealed in his word. May God reveal himself to you again as we journey through this beautiful meditation.

STEPHEN RAND

Sunday 10 November   **Psalm 119:1–6 (NIV)**

The secret of happiness

Blessed are those whose ways are blameless, who walk according to the law of the Lord. Blessed are those who keep his statutes and seek him with all their heart – they do no wrong but follow his ways. You have laid down precepts that are to be fully obeyed. Oh, that my ways were steadfast in obeying your decrees! Then I would not be put to shame when I consider all your commands.

Remembrance Sunday is not a day you would associate with blessing. Yet many soldiers read the Bibles they had with them at the front – during World War I, the Bible Society distributed more than nine million copies of scripture in over 80 languages to the armed forces on all sides. In 1918, 29-year-old Theo Chadburn wrote to his wife Lily from France, describing a Salvation Army meeting two weeks earlier: 'It was the best Easter Sunday night meeting I have ever spent. I was greatly blessed.' Two weeks later he died, (it is thought) rescuing colleagues from a burning building.

'Blessed' is such a Bible word, perhaps best known from the summary of Jesus' teaching in the beatitudes of the sermon on the mount. It can also be translated 'happy'. The search for happiness seems such a modern concern, and few people these days would go to the Bible to find the secret of happiness. (Sadly, few expect to find happy people in church.)

This first phrase of Psalm 119 could mean that God will bless those who keep his laws: 'Our Lord, you bless everyone who lives right and obeys your Law' (v. 1, CEV). It's a basic view of how God works: do what you're told, and I'll see you are rewarded. I prefer the more descriptive meaning: 'How happy are those whose way of life is blameless' (v. 1, CJB). Living in God's world God's way is the route to real happiness – there is a linguistic link between the words 'bless' and 'bliss'. This is a lovely translation: 'You're only truly happy when you walk in total integrity, walking in the light of God's word' (v. 1, TPT).

On this Remembrance Sunday, we give thanks for those who gave their lives for others – and for those who found blessing as they read their Bibles.

STEPHEN RAND

Monday 11 November   **Psalm 119:9–11 (NIV)**

Whole-hearted living

How can a young person stay on the path of purity? By living according to your word. I seek you with all my heart; do not let me stray from your commands. I have hidden your word in my heart that I might not sin against you.

The psalmist is wrestling with the reality that was opened up in the first verses of the psalm, yesterday's reading. If the secret of happiness is found in living in God's world God's way, how can that be achieved? How can the young person – indeed, anyone – stay on the path of purity?

The first answer seems little more than a repeat, a tautology: you keep doing the right thing by doing the right thing. But there is wisdom here. Much of our behaviour is habitual, so developing good habits makes it easier to keep doing the right thing. Bad habits can be catastrophically destructive of the 'path of purity'.

Then the heart becomes the focus. In the Bible, the heart is the essence, the core, of every individual. The heart thinks, remembers, reflects and meditates. It is the source of attitudes, words and actions. Jesus said, 'Where your treasure is, there your heart will be also' (Matthew 6:21).

The challenge and the key to living the right way is where our hearts, our whole lives, are focused. We must seek God with everything that we have and we are. Our overwhelming ambition must be to know God, to have our lives and actions informed by his word – that's why we hide it in our hearts. We take it in, we learn from it, it informs our whole being.

When I was a young boy, a friend of my father's visited our house. His name was Geoffrey Bull. A missionary in Tibet, he had been captured by the Chinese and undergone a lengthy ordeal of torture and brainwashing. I asked him how he had kept going. He answered that he had tried to fill his mind with all the verses of the Bible he could remember. The words he had hidden in his heart kept him faithful to his God.

Father God, help me to be wholehearted in my longing for you
and your presence in my life. Amen

STEPHEN RAND

Tuesday 12 November — Psalm 119:16 (NIV)

Delight

I delight in your decrees; I will not neglect your word.

The psalm keeps giving us these unlikely words and concepts. Today it is the idea that the writer 'delights' in the words of God. I wonder how you feel when you pick up your copy of *New Daylight*? (I just typed *New Delight* by mistake; now there's a thought!) I suspect that for many of us duty rather than delight is the dominant emotion, however well we writers do. It is a case of summoning determination that the writer expresses here: 'I will not neglect your word.'

I've done some research into the Hebrew word that is translated 'delight'. In Isaiah 66:12 it is rendered as 'dandled', meaning stroked and cuddled, a baby bounced on its mother's knee. That's a rich vision of delight – mother and baby sharing their joy together.

I can't claim that this is my daily experience of the Bible. But I'm glad and grateful for the times when, exploring a passage together with friends in a home group, I have made new discoveries that have given me genuine delight, or when getting to grips with the text, so I can say something meaningful when preaching the following Sunday or writing these notes, has given me joy. And some people have been kind enough to say they have shared in that when they have heard or read the result!

Dandling my little granddaughter Stella on my knee is definitely a source of delight to me. She doesn't always respond enthusiastically, but I don't give up, because she often does gurgle with her own enjoyment. The more we persevere in our engagement with the Bible, the more opportunities there are for delight to be the result.

Delight is a very definite feature of this psalm. Eight times the writer underlines that delight is one response to the word and words of God. I wonder if that is because words are the way we get to know someone, as they communicate with us. Words become the basis of relationship. Our delight in the Bible comes when it deepens our relationship with the God who loves us.

Loving Father, grant me more occasions when duty produces delight and deepens my relationship with you. Amen

STEPHEN RAND

Wednesday 13 November   **Psalm 119:18 (NIV)**

Eyes wide open

Open my eyes that I may see wonderful things in your law.

Yesterday my grandchildren came to visit and played one of their favourite games – hunt the thimble. They love the fact that Grandad has his eyes open, but he just can't see!

Many people have begun their daily Bible reading by making this verse their prayer. You could do worse! The meaning is surely linked to yesterday's verse – the more we discover wonderful things, the more delight we will experience. Notice that it is a prayer. Just as the existence of God's word is the result of his initiative, so the ability to understand, to see the wonderful things, is dependent on him. It doesn't come just from our own cleverness. That in itself is wonderful. Over the centuries and around the world, ordinary, even illiterate, people have found God through his word.

In Mexico City, I met a professor who wanted a group of uneducated slum-dwellers to discover the Bible for themselves, not simply learn about it from him. He got them to act out the stories from the gospels, then share with each other how they felt as they had got into the role of disciple, sower, good Samaritan and so on. There were opened eyes and great delight in those sessions.

There are two approaches to reading the Bible that, if focused on in isolation, lead to disaster. The first emphasises the mind: the Bible is worthy of rigorous academic study. The second underlines that we need God's Holy Spirit to help us understand the Bible. Both are true.

Rigorous academic study without God's Spirit becomes dry and lifeless. Far too many people know and experience God less after three years of a theology degree course! But a mindless reliance on God's Spirit to interpret scripture can lead to damaging, thoughtless behaviour. The caricature story to illustrate this is that of the person who prayed for guidance, opened their Bible at a random page, stabbed at a verse with their finger and read, 'Judas went and hanged himself' (see Matthew 27:5).

To behold wonderful things in God's word, we need to open our minds, use our brains and ask God to open our eyes and grant us understanding.

STEPHEN RAND

Thursday 14 November   **Psalm 119:19 (NIV)**

Not at home

I am a stranger on earth; do not hide your commands from me.

When I was a teenager – in a previous millennium – we often sang what to us was a new song, which I think we liked mostly for its bouncy tune. Checking the song's history now, I've discovered that it was an American gospel song made famous by Jim Reeves, among others. It began, 'This world is not my home, I'm just a-passing through.'

The song reflects a truth stated clearly – but rarely – in the Bible: 'This world is not our permanent home; we are looking forward to a home yet to come' (Hebrews 13:14, NLT). The psalmist says something similar on just one other occasion: 'Hear my prayer, O Lord!... Don't ignore my tears. For I am your guest – a traveller passing through' (Psalm 39:12, NLT). Just before his death, King David celebrated the generous gifts given for the building of the temple, and made this comment: 'We are here for only a moment, visitors and strangers in the land as our ancestors were before us. Our days on earth are like a passing shadow, gone so soon without a trace' (1 Chronicles 29:15, NLT).

The word that is used each time is the word that appears so often in the law of Moses when the people of Israel are repeatedly instructed to be generous to the 'stranger' living among them. Different translations use 'sojourner', 'foreigner', even 'alien'.

Here in Psalm 119 the writer feels alienated from the world around him, a stranger. It is, on the one hand, an uncomfortable situation. On the other, it is a reminder that God has been generous to us, and prepared a permanent, eternal home for us with himself. Paul wrote, 'You were without Christ, you were utter strangers to God's chosen community... But now, through the blood of Christ, you who were once outside the pale are with us inside the circle of God's love and purpose' (Ephesians 2:12–13, Phillips).

We may be strangers on the earth, just passing through. But the certain hope of our future inspires us to live for God now, fulfilling his commands in the world and for the people around us.

Help me to live every moment aware of your presence.

STEPHEN RAND

Friday 15 November **Psalm 119:28 (NIV)**

Worn out with sorrow

My soul is weary with sorrow; strengthen me according to your word.

All of our lives have their ups and downs. One of the most encouraging features of the psalms is that they reflect the whole range of life's experiences. The writers speak out of moments of great joy, but they are not afraid to also address God at their moments of deepest sadness.

I have no idea as I write this what your circumstances will be when you read it. I do know there is every likelihood that at least one reader will be in the midst of great grief. At least one will instantly recognise the experience as it is described in this translation, 'I am drowning in tears' (v. 28, GW).

My guess is that, if you are in the midst of this level of grief, there is little I can write that will offer immediate comfort. All I know is that there are those who will testify that they clung on to the fact that Jesus – who wept in Gethsemane and who cried out 'My God, my God, why have you forsaken me?' in his suffering on the cross (Matthew 27:46) – would never let go of them and never leave them. And he didn't.

There is no promise in the Bible that those who follow Jesus will be given a 'Get out of jail free' card every time they face suffering. It is likely that all but one of Jesus' closest friends was executed horribly. Paul's statement in Romans 8:35–39 was not that Christians would never experience 'trouble or hardship or persecution or famine or nakedness or danger or sword'; the best he could offer was that absolutely nothing 'will be able to separate us from the love of God that is in Christ Jesus our Lord.'

That is what God has promised. And the psalmist here, as he drowns in his tears, cries out, 'Strengthen me as you promised.' He knows that God can be trusted, that God always keeps his promises.

Lord, today we join in prayer for every reader who is facing suffering and grief right now. May they know your presence and your love surrounding them. Strengthen them as you have promised. Amen

STEPHEN RAND

Saturday 16 November — Psalm 119:49–56 (NIV)

Hope in the face of suffering

Remember your word to your servant, for you have given me hope. My comfort in my suffering is this: your promise preserves my life. The arrogant mock me unmercifully, but I do not turn from your law. I remember, Lord, your ancient laws, and I find comfort in them. Indignation grips me because of the wicked, who have forsaken your law. Your decrees are the theme of my song wherever I lodge. In the night, Lord, I remember your name, that I may keep your law. This has been my practice: I obey your precepts.

These verses echo a familiar theme of the psalms. The writer feels hemmed in, under pressure. He is facing personal abuse, being mocked unmercifully. This is a world where the wicked are thriving, while those who are trying to live the right way are belittled, marginalised and made to suffer. He uses various terms in the psalm to describe his difficulties: he faces 'scorn and contempt' (v. 22); he is 'smeared with lies' (v. 69); he is 'being persecuted without cause' (v. 86); 'Trouble and distress' have come upon him (v. 143), leaving him 'like a wineskin in the smoke' (v. 83).

But a feature of Psalm 119 is the way a determined response follows the description of his troubles. He perseveres, he keeps going. In this passage he affirms, 'I do not turn from your law'; 'I remember your name'; 'I obey your precepts.' The key to his perseverance lies in v. 49: 'you have given me hope.' However bleak the situation, he held on to the confidence that it would not always be like this. That's why he could also write, 'Your promise preserves my life' (v. 50).

This lesson was reinforced for me so often when I travelled with Tearfund. I met people in desperate circumstances, yet their faith was strong and hope burned strongly. I remember Hidenia in the Philippines, her eyes full of tears as she described how she had lost her three-month-old baby to measles. I asked her, 'What does knowing Jesus mean to you?' Her face changed. A smile formed through the tears. 'I know that one day I will be with him in heaven,' she said.

Life without hope is soul-destroying; hope itself can preserve life when all seems lost.

STEPHEN RAND

Sunday 17 November   **Psalm 119:72, 103 (NIV)**

Precious

The law from your mouth is more precious to me than thousands of pieces of silver and gold… How sweet are your words to my taste, sweeter than honey to my mouth!

These verses are strikingly countercultural in today's society. Can anything be more precious than wealth? Our whole society is orientated around money: the economy is a focus of the national news; politicians compete to convince us they will make us better off; gambling advertising dominates sporting television; and I'm always waiting behind someone buying lottery tickets in our corner shop when I pop in to buy the paper.

    It's easy to look at others; harder to examine ourselves. My family are always entertained by my devotion to vouchers and coupons. I enjoy a bargain, but just how obsessive am I about money? Am I generous and open-handed or tight-fisted (Deuteronomy 15:11)?

    The psalmist imagines that he has to choose between untold wealth and God's word. And he is convinced that being in touch with God – being guided by his word, learning more about him, building a relationship with him – is the more precious. It's so valuable, it tastes so sweet, that it is the focus of his life, his greatest priority.

    Jesus said, 'Be generous. Give to the poor. Get yourselves a bank that can't go bankrupt, a bank in heaven far from bank robbers, safe from embezzlers, a bank you can bank on. It's obvious, isn't it? The place where your treasure is, is the place you will most want to be, and end up being' (Luke 12:33–34, MSG). It's not about never missing your daily reading; it's not about becoming pious and other-worldly. It's about wanting to know God and know him more, so that we learn from him and live for him.

    In the parable of the sower, some seed fell among thorns. These are people who 'hear the word; but the worries of this life, the deceitfulness of wealth and the desires for other things come in and choke the word, making it unfruitful' (Mark 4:18–19).

Dear Lord, help me to keep discovering how precious and sweet your word is – and help me to be fruitful.

STEPHEN RAND

Monday 18 November — Psalm 119:105 (NIV)

Guidance

Your word is a lamp for my feet, a light on my path.

This is a beautiful and well-loved verse. Two simple but evocative images are brought together in a way that sums up why so many people love to read the Bible.

The first image – 'a lamp for my feet' – is intensely personal. The lamp is in my hand, its beam creating a pool of light just in front of me, showing clearly where my feet should go, making I sure I don't step in the puddle, trip over the kerb or miss the step. When surrounded by darkness, illumination is vital if we are to move forward with confidence and not be wrong-footed or stumble into difficulty, even disaster. God's word can fulfil that purpose in our lives.

Note that the light is for the feet. It is not a sunlamp to relax under, but a resource to enable us to move forward, one step at a time. Life with God is a life on the move, living with purpose. So many people think the Christian faith is simply about believing the right set of religious statements, such as the Apostles' Creed or the 39 Articles. But faith means putting belief into action, walking with God. The first name for Christians was people of 'the Way' (Acts 9:2).

This links to the second image: 'a light for my path'. This is the full blazing illumination of the sun – the same word as when 'God said, "Let there be light," and there was light' (Genesis 1:3). The path we should follow is as clear as day.

It doesn't always seem like that, does it? When I spoke at Christian events, large numbers always attended seminars on guidance. They wanted answers to the most important questions: where they should live, what job they should do, whom they should marry. I couldn't give them those answers, but I could point out that God's word gives a great deal of guidance on how to live, what attitudes we should bring to our work and how we should treat our spouse.

Loving Father, I need your guidance each day. Light my path as I read your word, so that I can follow you more closely.

STEPHEN RAND

Tuesday 19 November   **Psalm 119:130 (NIV)**

Illumination for the mind

The unfolding of your words gives light; it gives understanding to the simple.

In yesterday's reading, God's word was the light of guidance as we follow Jesus step by step. Today, light is linked to understanding. When we are struggling to make sense of a problem or a situation, we often say, 'Then the light came on,' to describe when understanding comes.

There are two levels of understanding that are illuminated by God's word. The first is the Bible itself. One of the best ways to make sense of the Bible is to read more of it. Terrible mistakes have resulted from a wrong emphasis on one phrase or verse; the more aware we are of the range and content of the whole Bible, the more likely we are to interpret a single verse wisely and correctly.

The second meaning is that the Bible can help us understand the wider world. I love teaching about the big picture of God's plan for the world and its people, which is revealed from the beginning of Genesis to the end of Revelation. Grasping the full scope of this helps to explain the Bible's specific stories, its poetry and its history, all of which illuminate each other.

The Hebrew word translated 'unfolding' is unique to this verse, found nowhere else in the Old Testament. It can be translated 'opening' – the link may be that doorways were often covered with a curtain, which when unfolded opened the doorway so light could flood in. In the New Testament the word used for 'revelation', God's revealing himself through his word, is one that literally means 'uncovering' or 'bringing to light'. It is also used to describe the 'appearing' of Jesus, when he will come in glory.

So again there are two levels of meaning in the phrase 'The unfolding of your words gives light.' The first is that we must open the Bible if we want to understand it; if the Bible remains closed, it will always be a closed book to us. The second is far less prosaic: as God's revelation of himself is unfolded in scripture, it will illuminate the whole of scripture.

Who are the 'simple'? Probably someone like me who struggles to understand the Bible. I certainly need illumination!

STEPHEN RAND

Wednesday 20 November   **Psalm 119:145–151 (NIV)**

Throughout the day you are near

I call with all my heart; answer me, Lord, and I will obey your decrees. I call out to you; save me and I will keep your statutes. I rise before dawn and cry for help; I have put my hope in your word. My eyes stay open through the watches of the night, that I may meditate on your promises. Hear my voice in accordance with your love; preserve my life, Lord, according to your laws. Those who devise wicked schemes are near, but they are far from your law. Yet you are near, Lord, and all your commands are true.

These are the words of someone under great stress, at the end of their tether. They are calling with their whole being, crying out for rescue, sleeping fitfully, waking early and shouting for help. The word used for 'cry' is the same word used for Jonah crying out to God from the belly of the great fish (Jonah 2:1) – situations do not come much more desperate than that.

The writer does what many people have done throughout history: he promises that if his anguished cry for help is answered, then he will become God's most committed, obedient servant. It's an understandable bargaining chip to offer but an incredibly difficult one to live up to; promises made under pressure are much harder to keep when the sun starts shining again. Mature Christians know God can't be manipulated – but maturity can crumble in the face of desperation!

Notice that even in desperation the psalmist knows to turn to God. God is the one who can save him. Two things convince him of that. The first is hope: he trusts God, and he therefore trusts his promises, one of which is that God is near: 'The Lord himself goes before you and will be with you; he will never leave you nor forsake you. Do not be afraid; do not be discouraged' (Deuteronomy 31:8). The writer was also convinced that God loved him. Holding on to that conviction has seen many through the severest storms of life.

Dear Lord, when I am at the end of my tether and close to despair, remind me of your promises and your presence.

STEPHEN RAND

Thursday 21 November   **Psalm 119:169–174 (NIV)**

This is my prayer

May my cry come before you, Lord; give me understanding according to your word. May my supplication come before you; deliver me according to your promise. May my lips overflow with praise, for you teach me your decrees. May my tongue sing of your word, for all your commands are righteous. May your hand be ready to help me, for I have chosen your precepts. I long for your salvation, Lord, and your law gives me delight.

The final section of Psalm 119 is a prayer that brings together many of the themes that have developed in the previous 21 sections.

First, the psalmist wants his cry to be heard. The phrase 'come before you' suggests the functioning of a royal court, where petitioners queue up in the hope of getting an audience with the king and a moment to press their case (see, for example, Esther 4:11). The Bible gives us confidence that when we pray we are not competing for the king's time, but that we are guaranteed a hearing by a loving Father.

He also wants understanding. He has read the words of God time after time, but without understanding the reading will be fruitless. This is a prayer we can echo every time we pick up *New Daylight*.

Then he is desperate for deliverance. Throughout the psalm, he has bemoaned the enemies surrounding him on every side. He is under threat; his life is at risk – he wants salvation. The story of the exodus had taught the Jewish people that God is in the rescue business; Jesus teaches us that he offers us eternal salvation – we are rescued to know his presence forever.

After all this, he praises God. The whole psalm is a curious mixture of peril, petition and praise. But the writer has discovered that worship is a wonderful antidote to worry. Praising God with fellow Christians builds confidence in God, his love and concern for us. Don't give up on worship when the going gets tough.

Finally, once again the psalmist rejoices that knowing God through his word gives him joy and delight.

How much are my prayers a mixture of praise and petition?

STEPHEN RAND

A life of praise

Let me live that I may praise you, and may your laws sustain me.

What is life for? In the 1640s, English and Scottish theologians drew up the Westminster Catechism, which became the core summary of Christian teaching for the Church of Scotland. The first question was: 'What is the chief end of man?' The answer: 'Man's chief end is to glorify God, and to enjoy him forever.'

The psalmist may simply be asking for his life to be spared, and promising to praise God if he grants his request. But it could also mean 'Give me life, so that I may praise you' (v. 175, GNT). That would resonate with the Westminster Catechism. We have life so that we can praise God.

I don't think that means endless singing and an overworked organist or worship band. We praise and worship God together in a Sunday service; we praise and worship God by living for him the rest of the week. That's when his laws offer guidance and his presence sustains us.

The commentary on the modern English version of the Westminster Shorter Catechism says, 'We can show his glory by doing everything in life as service to him. This means that God must be first in our lives; only as we know and love him can we truly please him.'

Jesus said, 'I have come that they may have life, and have it to the full' (John 10:10). The GNT puts it, 'I have come in order that you might have life – life in all its fullness.' The constant challenge is for the church to teach – and Christians to believe – that living God's way is not only the right way to live, but the best way, the most fulfilling way. We do this not by being more religious, but by being full of life.

I treasure a moment at university when a friend said to me, 'I have to drink several pints of lager to be as happy as you are all the time.' I've always opted for the most positive interpretation of this comment – and trust that I've carried a hint of its truth for the subsequent 50 years.

Help me to discover life in all its fullness, and live it in you and through you day by day.

STEPHEN RAND

Saturday 23 November   **Psalm 119:176 (NIV)**

All we like sheep

I have strayed like a lost sheep. Seek your servant, for I have not forgotten your commands.

This psalm has not been written by a spiritual giant, someone who lived a life that we could never aspire to. Rather it's been written by someone subject to doubt, prone to failure, under pressure – but determined to hang on, to keep going.

He finishes this long and complex poem with a prayer that comes from pathos rather than triumph: 'I have strayed.' The analogy is a common biblical one, rooted in the everyday life of a shepherd in the Middle East. Isaiah echoes the same thought: 'We all, like sheep, have gone astray, each of us has turned to our own way; and the Lord has laid on him the iniquity of us all' (Isaiah 53:6). Many Christians see this verse from Isaiah as summarising the gospel: because humanity had strayed from God, God took the initiative and sent Jesus into the world 'that the world through Him might be saved' (John 3:17, NKJV).

What's more, in asking 'Seek your servant', the writer anticipates the words of Jesus: 'What do you think? If a man owns a hundred sheep, and one of them wanders away, will he not leave the ninety-nine on the hills and go to look for the one that wandered off?' (Matthew 18:12) This not only emphasises the value that each individual has to God, but also hints at the deep truth that when we think we are seeking God, God is seeking us. Jesus said, 'For the Son of Man came to seek and to save the lost' (Luke 19:10).

I met someone recently who had been a convinced atheist, but at a time of crisis in their life went and sat down in the quiet of a deserted parish church. At that point they heard God speak to them, saying, 'I want you.' They had replied, 'Well, I don't want you,' but that was how their journey to faith began.

Dear God, thank you for this psalm that has celebrated the value of your word. Please keep seeking me, that I may know you more and live for you joyfully and effectively. Amen

STEPHEN RAND

Introduction

Glory

My computer tells me that the word 'glory' appears in the Bible 456 times. That is not including its cognates, 'glorify', 'glorified' and so on. Think, too, of all the hymns with 'glory' in the title or text, and (at the risk of over-egging the pudding) for those familiar with the *Book of Common Prayer*, one sings 'The Gloria' five times at morning prayer!

It would seem, then, that this notion of glory is an important one in our faith. However, when something is very familiar, there is the potential to accept it without really examining what is meant. With this in mind, for the next two weeks we are going to focus on glory and explore some of its meanings. But to begin to tease this out, we need to appreciate that the term is used in three ways.

First, the glory of anything is to do with its intrinsic worth, value or splendour; so when we talk of the glory of God, we are talking about the very essence of God – the characteristics of majesty, holiness, love, wisdom and power. Second, our response to God's glory is to reciprocate through our worship and everyday life. It is the Christian belief that we exist in order to glorify God. Finally, it is a further belief that through our efforts to offer God glory, we in turn share in that glory and become glorified both here on earth and in the life to come. Having said all that, because believing that Jesus is God, all three items listed above apply to Jesus, too.

It is perhaps worth concluding this introduction by noting that while 'glory' is a very familiar word to Christians – one that we use a great deal, almost without thinking – it is a word with a bit of weight behind it, a word with gravitas. The Hebrew is *kabod*, which comes from a root word carrying the notion of weight and heaviness. *Kabod* is used to describe the power and riches of a human being; applied to God it also tells of power, but power expressed through majesty and sovereignty.

Many of the passages we will look at are familiar, but that merely reinforces the notion that this concept of glory is at the heart of our faith.

GEOFF LOWSON

Sunday 24 November — **Psalm 19:1-6 (NRSV)**

The heavens are telling

The heavens are telling the glory of God; and the firmament proclaims his handiwork. Day to day pours forth speech, and night to night declares knowledge. There is no speech, nor are there words; their voice is not heard; yet their voice goes out through all the earth, and their words to the end of the world. In the heavens he has set a tent for the sun, which comes out like a bridegroom from his wedding canopy, and like a strong man runs its course with joy. Its rising is from the end of the heavens, and its circuit to the end of them; and nothing is hidden from its heat.

My small office overlooks the open countryside of the northern Pennines. I look up the valley, with smaller valleys snaking off to either side, and then the fells rise and tumble over each other. On a clear day, I can see a mountain called Cross Fell, which, at 2,930ft, is the highest point in the Pennine Chain. It is said that it takes its name because St Augustine of Canterbury climbed it and blessed it, but I wonder – it's a long walk from Canterbury!

As the seasons change, the full majesty of nature unfolds. And over it all is a magnificent sky; there are sunsets that would do justice to any holiday brochure and, with very little light pollution, starry nights really are starry. For me, the ultimate is a sunny morning with a crisp frost and snow-capped fells.

Psalm 19 opens quite unambiguously: creation shows forth the glory of its creator. As one gazes at the beauty of creation, no words are required. Yet, paradoxically, it speaks volumes.

But there is another aspect found here. Biblical thought often attributes to things and objects the ability to praise and glorify their creator. This is expressed in Osler's hymn, 'Praise the Lord, ye heavens adore him': 'sun and moon rejoice before him, praise him all ye stars and light.' And so it is in the passage above; not only is creation showing forth God's glory, but creation itself is offering glory to God. And it is doing it with joy.

God of glory, as David wondered at your creation,
may we too stand in awe and thanksgiving.

GEOFF LOWSON

Monday 25 November   Psalm 65:9–12 (NRSV)

Our bounteous God

You visit the earth and water it, you greatly enrich it; the river of God is full of water; you provide the people with grain, for so you have prepared it. You water its furrows abundantly, settling its ridges, softening it with showers, and blessing its growth. You crown the year with your bounty; your wagon tracks overflow with richness. The pastures of the wilderness overflow, the hills gird themselves with joy.

I was 14 when I first played the organ for the harvest festival service in the village. I remember clearly having to learn to play Psalm 65 from *The Cathedral Psalter*: 'Thou visitest the earth, and blessest it; thou makest it very plenteous.' Members of traditional church choirs may know the harvest anthem by Maurice Greene (1696–1755) which starts with those same words.

Yesterday's reading drew attention to the intrinsic glory of God and creation's witness to that; this passage makes us aware of God's ongoing goodness, which in itself is an expression of God's glory. This psalm may have been written to give thanks for a particularly good harvest, but it could equally have been a song to celebrate the spring rains. Whatever the case, it would be hard to better this poetic description of a fertile earth.

The use of the word 'visit' is interesting, as it expresses a recurring biblical theme – the notion that while God is ever present and active, there are times when he draws near in a particular way. Here, God is blessing the earth with his bounty, wonderfully expressed in the image of the wagon so laden with produce that its contents spill out on to the track.

When I played at that service all those years ago, the church was full to overflowing. Today, harvest festivals, even in the country, do not have the same impact. Growers perhaps rely more on technology and fertilisers than they do on God. But one real and positive change is that congregations and school assemblies put an emphasis on our unity with peoples in more distant places, both those who also share in creation's beauty and goodness and those who sadly don't.

God of glory, we share your bounty with brothers and sisters throughout the world. Help us make that sharing real.

GEOFF LOWSON

God in the cloud

Then Moses went up on the mountain, and the cloud covered the mountain. The glory of the LORD settled on Mount Sinai, and the cloud covered it for six days; on the seventh day he called to Moses out of the cloud. Now the appearance of the glory of the LORD was like a devouring fire on the top of the mountain in the sight of the people of Israel. Moses entered the cloud, and went up on the mountain. Moses was on the mountain for forty days and forty nights.

Today's passage draws attention to two familiar phenomena that are very much part of the biblical imagery associated with God's glory – cloud and light. In this case, a flame is within a cloud.

In the UK, clouds are familiar to us all, but in the Bible 'the cloud' is used in a specific way to denote God's presence and God's glory. We first meet this idea when we read of the pillar of cloud leading the people of Israel through the wilderness.

This passage, however, introduces us to something slightly more profound; it is the notion of the cloud settling or resting over the mountain. In Hebrew writing, there is a word to describe this: *shekinah*, which derives from a verb that means 'to settle' or 'to dwell'. The word is not found in the Old Testament, but emerges later in the writing of scholars to denote God's dwelling among his people.

Behind the notion of *shekinah* was the idea of divine transcendence – God's being too holy to be within human touch or understanding or, as the philosopher Immanuel Kant (1724–1804) put it, 'that which cannot be perceived or explored by human cognitive faculties'. Of course, the paradox for us is that this transcendent God, who cannot be approached or seen, becomes immanent in Jesus.

Back to the view from my window – common sense dictates that I cannot see the mountains every day because of clouds. But even though I cannot see them, I know that they are there.

Almighty God, open our eyes to your presence over and around us, even on those days when you seem hidden from our sight. For we know you are there.

GEOFF LOWSON

Wednesday 27 November   **John 11:1–4 (NRSV)**

Affection of the mind

Now a certain man was ill, Lazarus of Bethany, the village of Mary and her sister Martha. Mary was the one who anointed the Lord with perfume and wiped his feet with her hair; her brother Lazarus was ill. So the sisters sent a message to Jesus, 'Lord, he whom you love is ill.' But when Jesus heard it, he said, 'This illness does not lead to death; rather it is for God's glory, so that the Son of God may be glorified through it.'

In the verses following today's passage, we read that, after hearing that Lazarus was ill, Jesus delayed going back to see him, a perhaps rather surprising response. By the time Jesus did get to Bethany, Lazarus had been dead for four days. Jesus asked Martha to open the tomb, whereupon she said to him, 'Lord, already there is a stench because he has been dead for four days.' Jesus responded, 'Did I not tell you that if you believed, you would see the glory of God?' (John 11:39–40).

The mention of four days is significant because the Hebrew people believed that the spirit of the departed hovered around the tomb until the fourth day in the hope of re-entering the body; after that it finally left. The point being made is that Lazarus was, in the eyes of everyone there, beyond returning from the grave. And yet Jesus brought him back to life.

In our language we have two ways of using the verb 'to see'; it can mean seeing something with our eyes or it can mean understanding. Believe it or not, in New Testament Greek there are fourteen ways of using 'to see'! In this case, in verse 40, it means true comprehension and the perception of a spiritual truth — it also hints at 'affection of the mind'. All those present would see Jesus' action, but those with faith would see the truth beyond, and see it with affection. They would see God's glory. Yesterday we noted that our transcendent God becomes immanent in Jesus; today we see God's glory being shown through faith and belief in Jesus.

Strengthen our faith that we too may see God's glory.

GEOFF LOWSON

Thursday 28 November   **John 1:14, 16–18 (NRSV)**

God with us

And the Word became flesh and lived among us, and we have seen his glory, the glory as of a father's only son, full of grace and truth… From his fullness we have all received, grace upon grace. The law indeed was given through Moses; grace and truth came through Jesus Christ. No one has ever seen God. It is God the only Son, who is close to the Father's heart, who has made him known.

Very occasionally, I used to play a childish but effective illustrative trick on my congregations. In a sermon I would ask them to stand and then perhaps turn around, wave their arms and then sit down again. The point I was trying to make was that a word or words can make things happen. I would say, 'Please stand,' and they stood; 'Please turn around,' and they turned around. I did say it was childish.

From the beginning we read of God's word making things happen. 'God said, "Let there be light"; and there was light' (Genesis 1:3). Thus, God created the world by his word, and furthermore, when he spoke to human beings, he expected a response.

However, in this well-known passage, John develops a new and richer meaning; the word now becomes the Word – a unique person who shares the very being of God. It may be that this idea arose from John's reading of the book of Proverbs, which gives a poetic, personified picture of God's mind or 'wisdom'. He could also have been influenced by a contemporary, the philosopher Philo, who believed that God by his reason (*logos*) creates the world, organises it and communicates with it.

For John, these ideas came together and were fulfilled in the Son of God, who has been with the Father from eternity and shares in his work of creation. What a shift from our transcendent God! Here we have our immanent God – this Word has come among us and works with us. The glory of God is seen in Jesus and in his actions. The Word has become flesh to live among us.

We thank you for your word recorded in holy scripture; grant that through the written word we may behold the glory of the incarnate Word.

GEOFF LOWSON

Friday 29 November   **John 2:9–11 (NRSV)**

The bridegroom cometh

When the steward tasted the water that had become wine, and did not know where it came from (though the servants who had drawn the water knew), the steward called the bridegroom and said to him, 'Everyone serves the good wine first, and then the inferior wine after the guests have become drunk. But you have kept the good wine until now.' Jesus did this, the first of his signs, in Cana of Galilee, and revealed his glory; and his disciples believed in him.

What constitutes an ordinary wedding these days? I am not being cynical, but is it in church or a hotel or a registry office? Does the bride walk in to organ music or a Coldplay track? I rather like weddings to have an air of formality, but I did once give in to a delightful couple who wanted their spaniel to bring the ring up the aisle. I should have known better; the dog had a party trick – if someone said 'Bang', it rolled on its back and played dead. The bridegroom's mates knew this, and the dog never did get to the front. Fun was had by all.

I am assuming that the wedding at Cana began as an ordinary wedding, but then Jesus' intervention made it extraordinary. However, while the image of gallons of wine captures our imagination and even makes us smile, the real significance of the story lies elsewhere. There are references in the Old Testament to the Lord's being the husband of Israel; for example, 'the covenant that I made with their ancestors when I took them by the hand to bring them out of the land of Egypt – a covenant that they broke, though I was their husband, says the Lord' (Jeremiah 31:32).

What we have here is Jesus as the bridegroom coming to reclaim his bride; that is, the people of God. And with that comes transformative power – the ordinary becomes extraordinary. The wine running out describes the human condition, in that material things can only partially satisfy our needs. The glory of Jesus revealed in the story is not the power to change water to wine, but the power to give eternal life.

Consider when you have felt Christ's transforming power in your life.

GEOFF LOWSON

Saturday 30 November — **John 17:1–5 (NRSV)**

'Through!'

After Jesus had spoken these words, he looked up to heaven and said, 'Father, the hour has come; glorify your Son so that the Son may glorify you, since you have given him authority over all people, to give eternal life to all whom you have given him. And this is eternal life, that they may know you, the only true God, and Jesus Christ whom you have sent. I glorified you on earth by finishing the work that you gave me to do. So now, Father, glorify me in your own presence with the glory that I had in your presence before the world existed.'

Chapters 14–17 of John's gospel are known collectively as the farewell discourses. They cover the time immediately after the last supper, when we hear Jesus talking in great depth with his disciples and then moving on to offer a prayer to his Father; today's passage is the beginning of that prayer.

To understand fully what Jesus is asking, we need to hold in our minds that immediately after this, he was arrested in the garden and, as we know, his arrest led to the cross. We further need to recall that Jesus had earlier referred to the cross as his glorification: 'The hour has come for the Son of Man to be glorified' (John 12:23).

Jesus knew that he had done all he could to fulfil God's wishes through his actions and teaching, but there was one more step that would show God's love to the full: the cross.

In 1915, Francis Martin, a young private in the Royal Engineers Signals Service, painted a work called simply 'Through!' With a bit of perseverance you can find it on the internet (see the Royal Signals Museum shop). It depicts an engineer fixing a field telephone line, but just as he completed his task, so that essential messages could get through, he was shot. He sacrificed his life but made the connection so that the message was 'Through'.

But, of course, the cross was not the end; there was the resurrection to follow. For Jesus, the cross was the way back – the way back to the glory he had known before the world began.

Reflect upon how you visualise a glorified Christ.

GEOFF LOWSON

Sunday 1 December — Luke 9:28b–32 (NRSV)

Dazzling light

Jesus took with him Peter and John and James, and went up on the mountain to pray. And while he was praying, the appearance of his face changed, and his clothes became dazzling white. Suddenly they saw two men, Moses and Elijah, talking to him. They appeared in glory and were speaking of his departure, which he was about to accomplish at Jerusalem. Now Peter and his companions were weighed down with sleep; but since they had stayed awake, they saw his glory and the two men who stood with him.

I am sure that you will have used the Good News Translation at some stage; I mention this because it often uses the words 'dazzling light' instead of 'glory'. In today's passage we have Jesus 'dazzling white'.

This incident in Jesus' life is recorded in Matthew, Mark and Luke's gospels and it is known and celebrated in the Christian calendar as the transfiguration. The three accounts are all slightly different, but they have in common the people involved and the image of Jesus shining; Matthew's gospel says, 'his face shone like the sun' (Matthew 17:2).

Biblical scholars suggest that this is oldest of the epiphany stories about Jesus, older than the story of the manifestation to the Magi or the shepherds and older than the account of the voice at Jesus' baptism. But whatever the case, it tells of Jesus choosing to reveal his divine mission to Peter, James and John and to reveal himself in all his glory. And the importance and drama of this is reinforced by the appearance of Moses and Elijah, representing, respectively, the law and the prophets. Jesus shows himself as the fulfilment of both.

Luke alone writes that the disciples were sleepy. I wonder if that apparently inconsequential bit of information has something to say to us? Many of us lead lives that are weighed down in various ways: not enough time; things to worry about – you can add to the list, I'm sure. Perhaps we miss God's glory when it is before us because we are so preoccupied with other things. I am sure I do!

As we begin this new Christian year,
may we make God's 'dazzling light' known.

GEOFF LOWSON

The First Sunday of Advent

Monday 2 December   John 5:39–44 (NRSV)

Vainglory

[Jesus said,] 'You search the scriptures because you think that in them you have eternal life; and it is they that testify on my behalf. Yet you refuse to come to me to have life. I do not accept glory from human beings. But I know that you do not have the love of God in you. I have come in my Father's name, and you do not accept me; if another comes in his own name, you will accept him. How can you believe when you accept glory from one another and do not seek the glory that comes from the one who alone is God?'

What follows is part explanation and part confession – more of the former, I hope. There is a sense in which clergy must be actors. I don't mean that they pretend to be something they are not, but they are required to perform in one way or another. On Sunday morning, the congregation expect a good show – and the all-age service requires all sorts of performance skills. On a more serious note, the liturgy does have a dramatic element to it.

But herein lies the problem. One wants to put on a good show for all the right reasons, but there is a fine line between doing it for one's own glorification and channelling that glory towards God.

Self-glorification is exactly what Jesus is warning his disciples against in today's passage. Jesus was in the temple, having completed two more miracles, or signs, as John calls them: healing a royal official's son at Capernaum and then healing a paralytic at Bethsaida. The religious leaders tackled Jesus about his activity, particularly since these healings had taken place on the sabbath, and part of his response was to try to assure his critics that everything he did was not for self-glorification but for the glory of God. But more than that, he challenged his Judean critics to look at their own actions, because they were forever trying to outdo each other rather than working together to the glory of God.

O Lord, guide our hearts and minds when we are tempted in the direction of vainglory.

GEOFF LOWSON

Tuesday 3 December — Deuteronomy 16:18–20 (NRSV)

Justice and only justice

You shall appoint judges and officials throughout your tribes, in all your towns that the Lord your God is giving you, and they shall render just decisions for the people. You must not distort justice; you must not show partiality; and you must not accept bribes, for a bribe blinds the eyes of the wise and subverts the cause of those who are in the right. Justice, and only justice, you shall pursue, so that you may live and occupy the land that the Lord your God is giving you.

I recall a meeting in a vicarage in rural Cumbria many years ago; the incumbent (an overly serious man) kept a few animals, and in response to an enquiry about his livestock, he began to share his genuine worries about two drakes who were being rather amorous towards one another. An aged and wise priest in the corner looked up and said, 'Don't worry, my boy; there will be something about it in the book of Deuteronomy.' It still makes me laugh out loud to this day.

Deuteronomy (and Leviticus) are full of lists of dos and don'ts – rules for this and rules for that. Many people find the books tedious. But we must not be too dismissive, because underlying all the minute detail is a grand plan, which was to create a society that was fair and that honoured God. Today we might question some of the content, but I don't think we can argue with the notion of fairness and justice.

Deuteronomy 16 gives instructions for three annual pilgrimages that all males had to observe – the Passover, the Feast of Weeks and the Feast of Tabernacles. At these celebrations, as well as the required religious observance there was the responsibility of appointing people to certain positions; here we read specifically of the duty to appoint 'judges', but very importantly, there is the express instruction that fairness and justice must be foremost.

Among the attributes and characteristics of God, God's love of justice – indeed his insistence on justice – is a major expression of his glory.

'Injustice anywhere is a threat to justice everywhere'
(Martin Luther King, Jr).

GEOFF LOWSON

Wednesday 4 December   **Luke 4:16–19 (NEB)**

Pursuing justice

So he came to Nazareth, where he had been brought up, and went to synagogue on the Sabbath day as he regularly did. He stood up to read the lesson and was handed the scroll of the prophet Isaiah. He opened the scroll and found the passage which says, 'The spirit of the Lord is upon me because he has anointed me; he has sent me to announce good news to the poor, to proclaim release for prisoners and recovery of sight for the blind; to let the broken victims go free, to proclaim the year of the Lord's favour.'

The theme of justice is carried over into the New Testament and was a major part of Jesus' teaching and ministry. For over 20 years, I worked for the mission agency USPG. It was a wonderful time, and one of the great privileges and indeed great joys was meeting people from all over the world, listening to their stories and sharing in their journey, albeit in a small way.

This is a generalisation, but if one passage of scripture captured the imagination of many of the folks I met, it is this passage from Luke. If you came from apartheid South Africa, or war-torn Mozambique, revolutionary central America or a poverty stricken part of India or Africa, these words sang out: 'This message is for me!'

Luke tells of Jesus' time in the wilderness, also mentions his teaching in Galilee, but then these are the first words we hear Jesus speak as he began his ministry. We know from scripture that Jesus attended and taught in the synagogue regularly, but this is the only content we know of; it has often been referred to as his manifesto. Jesus is proclaiming a ministry of release, and it is release through him – note the repeated use of the word 'me'. And it is a message for the poor. We tend to define poverty in economic terms, but Luke uses 'poor' as an umbrella word for any sort of oppression.

Jesus expressed God's glory through his announcing good news to the poor by word and deed, and in so doing he glorifies us.

Almighty God, help us to proclaim the good news of your justice.

GEOFF LOWSON

Thursday 5 December — Psalm 96:1–7 (BCP)

O worship the Lord

O come, let us sing unto the Lord, let us heartily rejoice in the strength of our salvation. Let us come before his presence with thanksgiving and shew ourselves glad in him with psalms. For the Lord is a great God and a great King above all gods. In his hand are all the corners of the earth and the strength of the hills is his also. The sea is his, and he made it and his hands prepared the dry land. O come, let us worship and fall down and kneel before the Lord our Maker. For he is the Lord our God and we are the people of his pasture, and the sheep of his hand.

This passage will be very familiar to a generation who know the *Book of Common Prayer* Mattins service – indeed, it has been used from the early days of the early church. The beauty of the words speaks for itself, but the phrase 'the sea is his' is worth a special note. To the heathen the sea represented a power even older than the gods, so to claim that 'the sea is his' is a profound statement.

It is thought that this psalm was used as part of the great Festival of Tabernacles (*Sukkot* in Hebrew), which occurred each October. *Sukkot* had two themes – one was thanksgiving for the autumn harvest; the other was a re-enactment and renewal of the convent between God and his people. This call to worship was sung before the processions entered the temple, and it was a reminder that the response to God's bounty was to offer worship.

I recall with affection the parish priest throughout my childhood and teenage years. To anyone who observed, 'You don't have to go to church to be a Christian' (all clergy have heard that one), he would reply, 'You can grow tomatoes outside, but they don't do as well!' It still makes me smile, and I confess to having pinched it to use myself.

Worship is the one thing we can give to God that is of ourselves. Through worship, we acknowledge God's glory; we give God glory and we are glorified.

'Make our worship more worthy, our witness more effective and our lives more holy' (Frank Colquhoun).

GEOFF LOWSON

Friday 6 December | Acts 2:43–47 (NEB)

Awesome!

A sense of awe was everywhere, and many marvels and signs were brought about through the apostles. All whose faith had drawn them together held everything in common: they would sell their property and possessions and make a general distribution as the need of each required. With one mind they kept up their daily attendance at the temple, and, breaking bread in private houses, shared their meals with unaffected joy, as they praised God and enjoyed the favour of the whole people. And day by day the Lord added to their number those whom he was saving.

This passage is one of my favourites and I particularly like the translation from the New English Bible. The NEB was published in 1961, when I was a teenager, and subsequent generations probably do not appreciate the impact that this first modern English translation made.

But this is more than just a favourite passage. The words 'in common' (v. 44) are from the Greek *koinonia*, which can be translated as communion, community, fellowship, partnership or even solidarity. For me, the glory of God finds wonderful expression in *koinonia* – community with all those other nuances and all the associated activities: a sense of awe, marvels and signs, real sharing, worshipping together and enjoying one another's company while also, importantly, dovetailing with wider communities.

It is a clichéd joke that clergy will do anything to escape preaching on Trinity Sunday – all those analogies (a clover leaf; a camera tripod; water, steam and ice; a plaited rope) to try to get across the concept of three-in-one and one-in-three. But at the risk of boasting, I never worried about that, because for me the Trinity is an expression of perfect community, and the church should aspire to reflect that in the world. It is no accident that in the creeds we express our belief in the three persons of God, then conclude by affirming our belief in the church.

The glory of God expressed through the church community and overflowing into the rest of the world. Now there's a thought. It could catch on!

God of community, may we show forth your glory in our community and through our community.

GEOFF LOWSON

Saturday 7 December   **2 Corinthians 5:17–20 (NRSV)**

Over to us

So if anyone is in Christ, there is a new creation: everything old has passed away; see, everything has become new! All this is from God, who reconciled us to himself through Christ, and has given us the ministry of reconciliation; that is, in Christ God was reconciling the world to himself, not counting their trespasses against them, and entrusting the message of reconciliation to us. So we are ambassadors for Christ, since God is making his appeal through us; we entreat you on behalf of Christ, be reconciled to God.

A former colleague, and one of my dearest friends, is a white South African theologian who lives just outside Cape Town. I note her colour, because she was one of the many white South Africans who fought against apartheid in the decades leading to its end in 1991; but her campaigning meant she had to leave her home country and live in England for about 20 years.

Reconciliation is a notion that is central to our faith. I recall one of the definitions of mission is that it is about God's reconciling us to himself, reconciling human to human and reconciling humankind to creation. It is a good definition, albeit a bit clumsy.

One of the many things my friend taught me was to look carefully at the word 'reconciliation'. She felt that many people (like me) use it too easily; we use it in a way that is a bit too 'fluffy' (my word, not hers). If one has lived through apartheid or under some equally oppressive regime, then reconciliation has to involve more than hugs. There has to be real repentance, too, and then change.

While acknowledging completely the significance of reconciliation, my friend preferred to talk of 'transformation', and indeed this term and concept has come more to the fore in the past decade or so. Our mission is about transformation.

But note Paul's words: Christ has given us that ministry; he has entrusted us with that mission of reconciliation/transformation. Over to us. That is how we can acknowledge God's glory and give God glory.

'Let your light shine before others, so that they may see your good works and give glory to your Father in heaven' (Matthew 5:16).

GEOFF LOWSON

> Introduction

Making the most of Advent: 'The God who comes'

The whole story of the Bible can be viewed as an account of the ways God comes to us. From beginning to end, it tells of a creator who constantly 'turns up' in the life of his creatures. Granted, he calls them to come to him, but that is always after he has come to them. That is true, as we shall see, from the first two chapters of Genesis to the last chapter of Revelation. Our response is to be alert to his presence and responsive to his touch.

Advent simply means 'coming'. We say that the advent of a new manager transforms a business, because 'comings' often make a difference. Think of the coming of a new baby in a family. God's comings to us, his intervention in human lives and situations, certainly has made a difference, as we shall see in many of the examples in the next fourteen readings.

At the Advent season, Christians are called to reflect on probably the two most significant of all those comings: the one that happened 2,000 years ago in Bethlehem, and the one we are promised at the end of human history, when God's purposes will be finally and gloriously revealed. To 'make the most of Advent' is to keep ourselves alert to the dealings of a God who is not just a remote cosmic power or distant being, but a Father who endlessly chooses to visit his children and a God who actually wants to be with his creatures. He is not a distant source of cosmic power, but a Father looking for his children.

I have chosen for these readings not only occasions when God has come in spectacular fashion – parting the Red Sea, arresting Paul on the road to Damascus – but also when he came to ordinary people, to change their circumstances or solve their needs. And it's not as though these 'comings' stopped at the end of Revelation. Many of us are probably aware of moments in our own lives – of sorrow or joy, of anxiety or hope – when God has come to us. The message of Advent is that he came, that he comes and that he will come again.

DAVID WINTER

Sunday 8 December — Genesis 2:5b, 7–8 (NRSV)

The breath of life

For the Lord God had not caused it to rain upon the earth, and there was no one to till the ground… then the Lord God formed man from the dust of the ground, and breathed into his nostrils the breath of life; and the man became a living being. And the Lord God planted a garden in Eden, in the east, and there he put the man whom he had formed.

There are, of course, two stories of the creation in Genesis. The first is a magnificent, sweeping picture of light in darkness, order in chaos and the emergence of life, ending with the majestic statement that God created human beings in his own likeness and image. That is the cosmic story. In chapter 2, however, the situation is different. There is grass and trees and foliage – but no one to till it!

Then we have this simple, beautiful little cameo. The creator himself scoops up the dust of the earth, shapes a human being from it and then – what a moment! – 'breathes into his nostrils the breath of life' (v. 7).

Neither the first story nor this one are meant to be cosmological or biological accounts. They are truth beyond facts. This is the first 'coming' of God to his human creation, and his gift is priceless: life – not just existence, but self-conscious human life in all its majesty and mystery. Life itself is a divine gift. God stooped over that inert, lifeless body and breathed life into it and 'the man became a living being' (v. 7). If the first creation account is cosmic, this one is domestic.

It's worth noting that in both Hebrew and Greek 'breath' and 'spirit' are the same word. God's breath, then, is by definition the Holy Spirit, 'the giver of life'. 'Body, mind and spirit' are our trinity of being. All are gifts in creation. Jesus, of course, 'breathed' on the disciples in the upper room after his resurrection. The breath of God was once again, and in a new way, in human nostrils. That precious breath of God still comes to us.

'Breathe on me, breath of God, fill me with life anew'
(Edward Hatch, 1878).

DAVID WINTER

Monday 9 December   Genesis 9:8–9, 11–13, 16 (NRSV)

When troubles come

Then God said to Noah and to his sons with him, 'As for me, 'I am establishing my covenant with you and your descendants after you... I establish my covenant with you, that never again shall all flesh be cut off by the waters of a flood, and never again shall there be a flood to destroy the earth.' God said, 'This is the sign of the covenant that I make between me and you and every living creature that is with you, for all future generations: I have set my bow in the clouds, and it shall be a sign of the covenant between me and the earth... When the bow is in the clouds, I will see it and remember the everlasting covenant between God and every living creature of all flesh that is on the earth.'

The flood is over. Noah and his family are able to leave the ark. It is then that God reveals a momentous truth. It is starkly simple, but of profound significance. There will never be a flood or similar disaster that will destroy what he has made. What he says is very explicit: not that there will be no more floods (or other disasters) – they are part of the way the world is – but that they will not destroy what God has made.

Human life includes in its very nature the constant risk of unwelcome events – floods, earthquakes, volcanos and accidents. The rainbow, which God chose as the sign of his covenant, is a picture of human life as we know it: the bow is formed of rain and sunshine. In their different ways, they represent to the people of earth both what is good and sustaining and what can be dangerous and destructive.

In that kind of world, the one God has given us to live in for a while, we know that life inevitably involves joy and sorrow, tears and laughter, gain and loss. It is in those moments, like Noah's flood, that we find our creator coming to us.

'You can endure it,' Paul assured the Corinthians
(1 Corinthians 10:13, NIV). That is his covenant in action –
'struck down, but not destroyed' (2 Corinthians 4:9).

DAVID WINTER

Tuesday 10 December   Exodus 3:7–9 (NRSV, abridged)

Answering a call for help

Then the Lord said, 'I have observed the misery of my people in Egypt; I have heard their cry on account of their taskmasters. Indeed, I know their sufferings, and I have come down to deliver them from the Egyptians, and to bring them out of that land to a good and broad land, a land flowing with milk and honey… The cry of the Israelites has now come to me; I have also seen how the Egyptians oppress them.'

This incident – Moses at the burning bush – is not only a turning point in the story of the Bible but, without exaggeration, in the whole history of religious belief in the world. Everything that follows in this conversation is a kind of vivid trailer for what eventually happens. The Passover, crossing the Red Sea, the promised land and a new kingdom: this is a prophetic step in a journey that leads eventually to the incarnation, the cross and the kingdom of heaven.

Moses had fled from Egypt after killing one of the brutal Egyptian taskmasters and was tending his father-in-law's flock in the Sinai Desert. He saw a bush burning but not being consumed. He drew near to see more, and was told by God that he was on holy ground. God had a message for Moses – and this was it. The cries and prayers of the Hebrew people had been heard and God had come (note the verb) to deliver them from their slavery. The voice that Moses heard (we are not told how) was that of the God of their fathers, now identified as 'I AM', the one who simply 'exists', our eternal creator and sustainer. The Hebrew for 'I AM' sounds like the Hebrew word translated 'The Lord', which represents for Jews the holy and unique name of God.

Moses also discovered, reluctantly at first, that he and his brother Aaron would be the human agents of this rescue. The people had cried for help. God had heard their cry and was now coming to their rescue. The God who comes had come.

The story of our salvation is the story of the God who comes to us in our need. Help me, Lord, to be alert to your presence and open to your grace.

DAVID WINTER

Wednesday 11 December Exodus 16:13–16 (NRSV, abridged)

Giving us 'daily bread'

In the evening quails came up and covered the camp; and in the morning there was a layer of dew around the camp. When the layer of dew lifted, there on the surface of the wilderness was a fine flaky substance, as fine as frost on the ground. When the Israelites saw it, they said to one another, 'What is it?'… Moses said to them, 'It is the bread that the Lord has given to you to eat. This is what the Lord has commanded: "Gather as much of it as each of you needs… all providing for those in their own tents."'

If you are trying, as Moses and Aaron were, to shepherd a large group of people across a desert the size of Sinai, there are two things you will certainly need: access to water, and daily food. Already on their journey the Israelites have begun to doubt their leaders' ability to deliver these essentials. They have watered at various oases. The complaint now is about their diet – such as it was. These verses record two events: one appears to be a natural one; the other, one of the foundation miracles of scripture.

They had lacked fresh meat on their journey. Now an obliging flock of quails descended on their camp, to provide a welcome supper. Then in the morning, the ground was covered by a flaky substance they had never seen before. 'What is it?' they asked – and instantly gave it its name. '*Manhu*' was what they said – 'manna' or 'wotsit', if you like. Moses then identified it. This was the food the Lord (Moses again uses the name from Exodus 3:15) had given them to eat, and it would be available every day except the sabbath until they reached their destination. Detailed instructions followed about how they were to gather, share and use it. A new word and a new concept had entered the history of faith.

Scholars have wondered what manna was – some think a secretion from the bark of some desert trees. That is irrelevant – most of the biblical miracles involve the use or transformation of something that already exists. God fed his people on their journey to the promised land, and he still does.

'Give us this day our daily bread,' we pray, and so he does.

DAVID WINTER

Thursday 12 December — Ruth 1:15–17 (NRSV)

God comes through human love

[Naomi] said, 'See, your sister-in-law has gone back to her people and to her gods; return after your sister-in-law.' But Ruth said, 'Do not press me to leave you or to turn back from following you! Where you go, I will go; where you lodge, I will lodge; your people shall be my people, and your God my God. Where you die, I will die – there will I be buried. May the Lord do thus and so to me, and more as well, if even death parts me from you!'

These words were spoken over 3,000 years ago, but they still resonate with enormous emotion. Ruth is speaking to her mother-in-law, Naomi, resisting the older woman's suggestion that she should return to her native Moab to find a husband. Reluctantly her sister Orpah has agreed to do so, but in a statement of total commitment, Ruth pledges herself to the elderly widow. Ruth, too, was a widow, as was Orpah, all three having lost their husbands in Moab, where Naomi had gone during a famine in Judah.

Ruth, a Moabite, makes it very clear in this beautiful act of commitment that she is not making her decision simply on emotional grounds. She has thought of the consequences: your people will be my people and your God, my God. Then, in a solemn vow, she invokes 'the Lord' (that name again).

In due course, Ruth did marry – a kinsman and landowner called Boaz. They had a son, Obed, who was the father of Jesse and grandfather of David, the great king. I think it's significant that in the family life of David, and hence of Jesus, was a woman from Moab, a Gentile, an immigrant, as we would say now; there she is in the family tree (Matthew 1:5–6). It is even more wonderful that God intervened in this tragedy of bereavements through an act of loving commitment.

Human love embraces all kinds of commitment. Help me, Lord, not to hold back in telling people how much I appreciate them.

DAVID WINTER

Friday 13 December   1 Kings 19:13–15a, 18a (NRSV)

When we are discouraged

When Elijah heard it, he wrapped his face in his mantle and went out and stood in the entrance of the cave. Then there came a voice to him that said, 'What are you doing here, Elijah?' He answered, 'I have been very zealous for the Lord, the God of hosts; for the Israelites have forsaken your covenant, thrown down your altars, and killed your prophets with the sword. I alone am left and they are seeking my life, to take it away.' Then the Lord said to him, 'Go, return on your way to the wilderness of Damascus… Yet I will leave seven thousand in Israel, all the knees that have not bowed to Baal.'

Elijah was recognised as the greatest of the Hebrew prophets (he stood with Moses beside Jesus at the transfiguration). Yet here we see him at his weakest, discouraged and desperate. It is a touching reminder that the Bible is ruthlessly honest, even about its greatest heroes. Elijah, put simply, was at the end of his tether. The king, Ahab, egged on by his wife, Jezebel, was openly supporting the pagan religion of Baal – and had threatened Elijah with death. The prophet's whole life's work was being destroyed. The people were turning to false gods. What had gone wrong? And why didn't God do something?

In our own lesser roles amid all the endless changes and chances of life, most of us have probably felt like this at some time or other. Churches are empty; there's blasphemy on the TV and there is no respect for Christian standards and values. What has gone wrong? And why doesn't God do something?

In just that situation, God came to Elijah. The conversation started with a question, 'What are you doing here'? Then a correction: 'It's not as bad as you think; there are many who have not bowed the knee to Baal.' And finally a command to 'Go' and get on with his God-given calling. Great things lay ahead, though he might not be part of them.

The earthquake, wind and fire must give way to the sheer silence of the divine voice. God's purpose will be fulfilled. All shall be well!

DAVID WINTER

Saturday 14 December — Luke 2:9–12 (NRSV)

Poor shepherds

Then an angel of the Lord stood before [the shepherds], and the glory of the Lord shone around them, and they were terrified. But the angel said to them, 'Do not be afraid; for see – I am bringing you good news of great joy for all the people: to you is born this day in the city of David a Saviour, who is the Messiah, the Lord. This will be a sign for you: you will find a child wrapped in bands of cloth and lying in a manger.'

We have seen how God's 'comings' often take us by surprise – Moses at the burning bush; Elijah on Mount Carmel – but this surpasses them all. Joseph and his pregnant wife are duly in Bethlehem (thanks to a Roman edict) and we are ready for the main event. So what comes next?

There were shepherds living in the fields, thinking only about their watchful rest through the long night ahead. Their quiet evening was suddenly interrupted by bright light and the voice of an angel. No wonder they were afraid.

The message they received was no less astonishing than the heavenly spectacle. This day would be the one their people had prayed and longed for through at least a thousand years. The Messiah was to be born in Bethlehem – just down the hill. But there was one more surprise. How would they recognise this special baby, a descendant of the great king David and God's appointed Saviour? Simple! He'll be wrapped in bands of cloth (not exactly regal) and lying in a feeding trough (barely civilised). The world-changing message delivered, the angelic vision disappeared.

Sometimes we say that a certain event makes a 'statement'. This one certainly did. The son of Mary would indeed be the Messiah, but not at all the warrior monarch that people expected would come to drive out the Romans and return sovereignty to the Jewish people. This Messiah, all through his life right up to his death, turned expectations upside down. He came for the poor, the weak and the helpless. He came to save sinners. This is how God comes as a Saviour.

When the shepherds reached the stable, they brought with them the whiff of the sheep pen. That's what we mean by incarnation: true God being truly human.

DAVID WINTER

Sunday 15 December — Matthew 14:22–27 (NRSV)

For those in peril on the sea of life

Immediately he made the disciples get into the boat and go on ahead to the other side, while he dismissed the crowds. And after he had dismissed the crowds, he went up the mountain by himself to pray. When evening came, he was there alone, but by this time the boat, battered by the waves, was far from the land, for the wind was against them. And early in the morning he came walking towards them on the lake. But when the disciples saw him walking on the lake, they were terrified, saying, 'It is a ghost!' And they cried out in fear. But immediately Jesus spoke to them and said, 'Take heart, it is I; do not be afraid'.

Many years ago, I was preaching on this story, which was the gospel for the day. I watched the congregation as it was read aloud and started my sermon with a request: would anyone who, while the gospel was read, thought 'He didn't, did he?' please raise their hand. No one did, until I pressed them to be honest with themselves. Slowly some hands went up and then more. Of course, they did. We are people of a scientific age. We know the physics.

I assured them that those who first heard that story would not have asked, 'Did it happen?' but 'What does it mean?' When reading it today, the second question is still the most relevant. Of course, the divine Son of the creator could walk on water (or fly) if he needed to. This story is not about a superman who can walk on lakes, but about a Saviour who comes to his friends when they are in desperate need.

They thought he was a ghost. He wasn't – the words are very strong: 'Do not be afraid. It is I.' Those last three words in Aramaic (the language of Jesus) are the holy name of God, 'I Am.' The one who came to those frightened sailors was the one who loved them and would die for them.

The sea is often used as a metaphor for the storms and setbacks of life. Jesus came to his friends walking across the very cause of their distress. The same Saviour still says, 'It is I. Do not be afraid!'

DAVID WINTER

Monday 16 December · John 20:13b–16 (NRSV, abridged)

In times of loss

[Mary said,] 'They have taken away my Lord, and I do not know where they have laid him.' When she had said this, she turned round and saw Jesus standing there, but she did not know that it was Jesus. Jesus said to her, 'Woman, why are you weeping? For whom are you looking?'... She said to him, 'Sir, if you have carried him away, tell me where you have laid him, and I will take him away.' Jesus said to her, 'Mary!' She turned and said to him in Hebrew, 'Rabbouni!' (which means Teacher).

At some time in the past, Jesus had cast 'seven demons' out of Mary Magdalene (Luke 8:2), the New Testament's description of what we could call a serious emotional or moral affliction. She became a devoted disciple and stood at the cross alongside his mother on that dark and bitter Friday. There is absolutely no doubt that she was devoted to Jesus and dependent on him.

And here we have her at the absolute depths of despair. Not only is her beloved Teacher and Lord dead, but his body has disappeared from the tomb where she had helped to lay him. A kind man, whom she took to be the gardener, asked her why she was weeping and for whom she was looking. Her reply is heart-rending: 'If you have carried him away, tell me where you have laid him, and I will take him away' (v. 15). His reply was one word: her own name, 'Mary'. The 'gardener' was Jesus!

That one word was enough. She made to embrace him, but he told her not to touch him – his resurrection was not yet fulfilled (John 20:17). But with joy she went off to find the other disciples, announcing to them, 'I have seen the Lord' (20:18). So this woman, once in the grip of some nameless evil, was now the apostle to the apostles. No wonder the church has always honoured her – the 'other Mary'.

My name is my individuality. The first word spoken by the risen Christ was a name, confirming that Mary was a precious individual in the family of God.

DAVID WINTER

Tuesday 17 December   **Luke 24:31–32 (NRSV)**

In moments of disillusionment

Then their eyes were opened, and they recognised him; and he vanished from their sight. They said to each other, 'Were not our hearts burning within us, while he was talking to us on the road, while he was opening the scriptures to us?'

I am pretty sure this story concerns Mr and Mrs Cleopas, but I'll leave you to do the detective work. Disciples of Jesus, they were making their way home to the village of Emmaus when they were joined by a stranger. They were so unhappy that he asked them what was wrong. They then recounted their experience of the crucifixion of Jesus. 'We had hoped,' they said, 'that he was the one to redeem Israel' (v. 21). What a sad sentence: 'we had hoped', but their hopes had been dashed.

The stranger, in fact the risen Christ, rebuked their doubts and took them through all the Hebrew scriptures, proving that what had happened to Jesus was consistent with the eternal purposes of God. When they arrived at their house, they invited him to stay and a meal was served. They asked him, as their guest, to bless their meal. He took the bread and broke it – and that's where our reading starts.

I love this story, because it encapsulates the two most frequent ways in which God 'comes' to us now, the Bible and Holy Communion (the 'breaking of bread'). That was when they recognised Jesus – like Mary Magdalene had done, they had failed to recognise him at first. What excited the couple at first was the memory of the Bible study they had shared on that seven-mile walk. Disillusionment was banished. Hope was restored. Their hearts 'burned within them', as the inspired teaching was carefully unfolded. Probably many of us have had moments when we have heard the scripture read or preached and we have had a similar moment of glorious comprehension.

Mr and Mrs Cleopas had the Messiah himself to unfold the old, old story – beginning with Moses. Today we have the Holy Spirit to do the same for us.

As the risen Christ opened their minds to the truth and their eyes to his presence, so the living Word comes to us every Sunday.

DAVID WINTER

Wednesday 18 December   **Acts 2:17–18, 21 (NRSV)**

God comes – for everyone

'In the last days it will be, God declares, that I will pour out my Spirit upon all flesh, and your sons and your daughters shall prophesy, and your young men shall see visions, and your old men shall dream dreams. Even upon my slaves, both men and women, in those days I will pour out my Spirit; and they shall prophesy… Then everyone who calls on the name of the Lord shall be saved.'

In the course of these readings we have seen God coming to us through his Spirit in ever-growing ways. He breathed the Spirit into the nostrils of a solitary man at creation. His Spirit came upon seers and prophets in the history of Israel. The Spirit came upon Jesus at his baptism, 'like a dove' (Matthew 3:16). In the upper room, Jesus breathed on the disciples and said, 'Receive the Holy Spirit' (John 20:22). And now, at Pentecost 40 days later, the Spirit is 'poured out' on the disciples. Now, in the words of Peter, the day has come when the Holy Spirit will be poured out on 'all flesh' (v. 17) – yes, Gentiles, aliens, people of other tribes and languages. The Spirit of God is free to work anywhere and everywhere.

The subsequent history of the church bears this out. Slowly at first, but as the centuries pass, more and more widely, we have discovered (as Peter himself did) that 'God does not show favouritism' (Acts 10:34, NIV). The Spirit of God cannot be contained any longer. The whole world and every living being is the Spirit's mission field. Men and women will 'see visions' and receive the truth – and share it.

Jesus said he would send his disciples a *parakletos* – a word variously translated as 'comforter', 'helper' and 'advocate'. Absolutely literally, the word means 'alongside-helper' – *para* we know as alongside and *kletos* is helper. That is what we have as the gift of God, and this is what Pentecost is all about. If the world needs help – and it surely does – we have the ever-present Spirit of God at hand.

Paul said that the love of God is 'poured into our hearts through the Holy Spirit, who has been given to us' (Romans 5:5, NIV). What a thought!

DAVID WINTER

Thursday 19 December   **Matthew 18:18–20 (NRSV)**

God comes – when we agree

'Truly I tell you, whatever you bind on earth will be bound in heaven, and whatever you loose on earth will be loosed in heaven. Again, truly I tell you, if two of you agree on earth about anything you ask, it will be done for you by my Father in heaven. For where two or three are gathered in my name, I am there among them.'

It's impossible to speculate about Jesus' view of how the church his disciples would found might develop in the future. Did the Galilean carpenter's son foresee the vast worldwide movement of over a billion people who would one day gather in his name? What he did foresee, and warn his disciples about, was the destructive power of disagreement. Even among the Twelve there were disputes, and it wasn't long into the story of the early church that open discord divided those who should have been united. The last great prayer of Jesus was that they should be 'one', perhaps because he knew the negative effects of division. This passage begins with the danger of unkind words (Matthew 18:10). It ends with a remarkable promise to those who live together in harmony.

We all know how bitter and destructive rows and feuds in a church can be. We know we are called to unity, love and peace, but our harmless disagreements can easily become disagreeable and then seriously destructive. Learning to live with difference is part of mature discipleship. Finding ways to agree with our fellow Christians brings blessings.

And here Jesus sets out the extent of that blessing. Agree about what you are asking for, and your prayers will be answered. But much more: where 'two or three', or two or three hundred, live in Christian agreement, Jesus says he will be 'among them'. After all, we are supposed to be his body. I don't think Jesus wanted followers who simply put up with anything! If so, he would never have made Peter the leader of the apostles. But he does want us to disagree in love (that is not a contradiction). Then he will share our true unity and love.

I may prefer one hymn, and you another, but there's no reason why we shouldn't sing both of them!

DAVID WINTER

Friday 20 December   **Matthew 28:18–20 (NRSV)**

God comes, so that we can go

And Jesus came and said to them, 'All authority in heaven and on earth has been given to me. Go therefore and make disciples of all nations, baptising them in the name of the Father and of the Son and of the Holy Spirit, and teaching them to obey everything that I have commanded you. And remember, I am with you always, to the end of the age.'

This, of course, is the end of the great commission, the final instructions from Jesus to his followers before his departure. It has formed an agenda for countless generations of Christians. This is what we are meant to be doing – going into all the world and making disciples from every nation. Jesus tells them to 'go', but they are going only because he has come. And many have 'gone' – literally to the ends of the earth. But we can 'go' right where we are – to that neighbour who is so anxious, to that single mum who can't cope, to that homeless man who sleeps outside Tesco. We can 'go' with Christian love and understanding. And, of course, we can 'go' to the ends of the earth by supporting the work of the gospel all over the world by our giving and our prayer. It's interesting that Jesus calls his followers to make disciples, not converts. A conversion is often sudden and dramatic. Discipleship is long-term, gradual and progressive.

But there, at the very end of our reading, is the ultimate assurance: 'Be clear, I am with you always to the end of the age.' We go, and he still comes – to be with us on the journey. What a wonderful idea! Whatever road you take (even at times the wrong one), I shall be with you, says Jesus, and right to the 'end of the age', the final cosmic curtain.

'May the road rise up to meet you.
May the wind be always at your back.
May the sun shine warm upon your face,
the rains fall soft upon your fields
and until we meet again,
may God hold you in the palm of his hand'
(Traditional Irish blessing).

DAVID WINTER

Saturday 21 December — Revelation 22:16–17, 20 (NRSV)

The final coming

'It is I, Jesus, who sent my angel to you with this testimony for the churches. I am the root and the descendant of David, the bright morning star. The Spirit and the bride say, 'Come.' And let everyone who hears say, 'Come.' And let everyone who is thirsty come. Let anyone who wishes take the water of life as a gift… The one who testifies to these things says, 'Surely I am coming soon.' Amen. Come, Lord Jesus!

This series of readings is entitled 'Making the most of Advent: the God who comes'. Here, at the very end of the Bible, we come face-to-face with the final coming, the one we assert in creed and liturgy: 'He will come again to judge the living and the dead.' I suspect many modern Christians don't feel at home with what we call the second coming. We churchgoers are happy to assert our faith in principle, but are agnostic as to how, when and even why it might happen. After all, even in the first century some Christians were having their problems about it (see 2 Peter 3:1–5).

The New Testament language on this subject is not factual but 'apocalyptic'. This doesn't mean (as news headlines suggest) scary, but simply 'revealed'. Jesus spoke of it, and here we have a reassuring glimpse of the wide-open gates of the kingdom of heaven – 'let everyone who is thirsty come' (v. 17). But behind all the visions there is a recurrent theme, what the Bible calls the 'day of the Lord'. This is not born of dreadful wars or plagues of locusts, but of the loving purpose of God. Eventually – and no one knows when – his glorious creation will have fulfilled its divine purpose. The hungry, thirsty and seekers will all have been gathered in. It will be time for a new kind of living, what Jesus called 'the kingdom of God'.

It is in the Bible and we sing it in a well-known hymn:
'When the earth shall be filled with the glory of God as the
waters cover the sea' (Arthur Ainger, 1894).
That's what we mean by this day of our Lord.

DAVID WINTER

Introduction

Christmas in Matthew

Being of an anxious disposition, I start to worry about the church nativity play in the middle of August, just after Holiday Club has ended, in fact! For many children, this will be the next time they visit the church, and the challenge of how to make the Christmas story interesting and accessible to each new generation is a mighty task. I have told the story in many different ways – from the viewpoint of Joseph or the wise men, narrated by a shepherd – or the donkey. We have included refugees, snails, real babies and over 100 knitted sheep in our efforts to share the wonderful news that Christ's birth is for all people, for all time. Each of these versions has included the same elements made familiar to all of us from plays, carols, sermons and stories, but each has been adjusted to the times and the audience, the community and its preoccupations.

And so it has been through the centuries, as hymns and carols change in emphasis, as traditions grow or become forgotten. It is interesting, therefore, to examine the story as told in just one gospel, to explore through one writer's eyes the events of the nativity and to notice which details are included and which are not seen as important.

For the next ten days, the story of Jesus' birth will unfold according to Matthew, beginning with his lengthy description of the generations back as far as Abraham, and ending with the family's arrival in Nazareth. We will explore Matthew's concern to show how Jesus' birth has been anticipated for generations and how the words of the prophets are fulfilled in the events of the nativity. The focus of Matthew is upon Joseph rather than Mary and upon the visit of the wise men rather than that of the shepherds. He doesn't flinch from the dark consequences of Jesus' birth, but shares with us the horror of Herod's cruelty and cowardice. It is a challenging version but above all a hopeful one, and I hope you find it interesting and rewarding as you begin this Christmas season.

SALLY WELCH

Sunday 22 December   **Matthew 1:1–6a (NRSV)**

Links in a chain

An account of the genealogy of Jesus the Messiah, the son of David, the son of Abraham. Abraham was the father of Isaac, and Isaac the father of Jacob, and Jacob the father of Judah and his brothers, and Judah the father of Perez and Zerah by Tamar, and Perez the father of Hezron, and Hezron the father of Aram, and Aram the father of Aminadab, and Aminadab the father of Nahshon, and Nahshon the father of Salmon, and Salmon the father of Boaz by Rahab, and Boaz the father of Obed by Ruth, and Obed the father of Jesse, and Jesse the father of King David.

Oh dear! Of all the ways to begin the greatest story of all time, a tale of hope and disaster, cruelty and ultimate triumph, a recitation of the hero's ancestors seems to be one of the most pedestrian. Luke begins by reassuring us about his careful study of exactly what took place; Mark is eager to share 'the good news of Jesus Christ', and plunges directly into the action. John takes us on a lyrical journey back before the beginning of time, when 'the Word was with God, and the Word was God'. But Matthew simply plods along in a series of 'begats', as the King James Version has it.

Why does he do this? Perhaps it is merely a literary device, lulling us with its rhythms and names so that the endless surprise of Christ will have a greater impact. Perhaps Matthew is trying to convince his doubting listeners, to reassure them that this Jesus, whose ancestry can be traced back to David, holds all the credentials for being the fulfilment of the prophecy, truly a member of the race of Israel, the children of God.

Perhaps, also, Matthew wants to show that Jesus is joining what has gone before, like links in a golden chain, leading the generations who have strived, each in their turn, to turn away from sin and work towards redemption. In this he offers us an invitation to do the same, to become true members of that family whose aim is restoration and life in all its fullness for all people.

Heavenly Father, may I be a part of the 'chain of glory', whose links are forged in heaven.

SALLY WELCH

Monday 23 December   **Matthew 1:12–16 (NRSV)**

'Who is called the Messiah'

And after the deportation to Babylon: Jechoniah was the father of Salathiel, and Salathiel the father of Zerubbabel, and Zerubbabel the father of Abiud, and Abiud the father of Eliakim, and Eliakim the father of Azor, and Azor the father of Zadok, and Zadok the father of Achim, and Achim the father of Eliud, and Eliud the father of Eleazar, and Eleazar the father of Matthan, and Matthan the father of Jacob, and Jacob the father of Joseph the husband of Mary, of whom Jesus was born, who is called the Messiah.

The recitation of genealogy is broken by the only historical statement that Matthew makes here: 'after the deportation to Babylon' (v. 12). These few words remind the reader that Israel's relationship with Jerusalem – the city of David, the city where God had his dwelling place, the home of the ark of the covenant and the heart of faith – had been ripped apart when the city was invaded and its people taken hostage to Babylon. The cause of this was the sin of the people, their abandonment of the true way of life and of God. When Israel disrupted their relationship with God, everything else was disrupted and challenging times followed. The hope of Israel lay with the return of the redeemer, the longed-for Messiah.

Generations later, with the promised land occupied, the children of Israel a subjugated nation, this Messiah at last appears, born to Mary, wife of Joseph, son of Jacob. Matthew makes no bones about this – there are no angels at this stage, no wise men come from the east to validate the announcement, simply a bald statement of belief. More than belief – a truth felt with every fibre of the writer's being.

Matthew's gospel is not a gentle exploration of the possibilities of Jesus, such as offered by Luke, nor a challenge, like that of Mark, to take the facts of Christ's life and decide on an individual level whether to believe or not. Matthew writes from faith and with faith, unswerving, rock solid, straightforward as the man himself must surely have been.

Jesus Christ, Messiah, give me the gift of faith as sure as Matthew's, that I may follow you with joy and assurance.

SALLY WELCH

Tuesday 24 December — Matthew 1:19–21, 24a (NRSV)

A righteous man

Her husband Joseph, being a righteous man and unwilling to expose her to public disgrace, planned to dismiss her quietly. But just when he had resolved to do this, an angel of the Lord appeared to him in a dream and said, 'Joseph, son of David, do not be afraid to take Mary as your wife, for the child conceived in her is from the Holy Spirit. She will bear a son, and you are to name him Jesus, for he will save his people from their sins'… When Joseph awoke from sleep, he did as the angel of the Lord commanded him.

What does it mean to be 'righteous'? The Cambridge dictionary defines it as 'morally correct or virtuous'. In slang usage it has connotations of excellence. Certainly it is an attribute of the highest kind, implying a person of upright and noble living who not only tries to do the good and right thing at all times but usually succeeds as well.

In this narrative, however, the very excellence of Joseph's nature leads him into difficulty. The righteous man in those times, the man of excellent moral character, when faced with a fiancée who is already expecting a baby, would of course be unable to proceed with the marriage; but he would act kindly towards the unhappy woman and send her to live quietly somewhere so that she would not bring shame on herself and her family. Being a righteous man, this is the course of action upon which Joseph decides.

But this decision, and indeed Joseph's entire life, is overturned by the visit of an angel to him in a dream. This angel gives Joseph a new definition of a righteous man – that is, someone who cares for a child who is not his own, and who supports the family while strange, wonderful and terrible things happen to it. With no warning or preparation, Joseph plays his low-key but vital part in the miraculous story of redemption that unfolds before him, maybe not understanding it all, but remaining constantly obedient to the will of God. Perhaps that, after all, is what it means to be righteous.

Lord God, make me righteous in your sight. Amen

SALLY WELCH

Wednesday 25 December   **Matthew 1:18, 24b–25 (NRSV)**

Doing God's work – quietly and simply

Now the birth of Jesus the Messiah took place in this way. When his mother Mary had been engaged to Joseph, but before they lived together, she was found to be with child from the Holy Spirit… [Joseph] took her as his wife, but had no marital relations with her until she had borne a son; and he named him Jesus.

Throughout my 20 years as a parish priest, my favourite Christmas service has been the one at 8.00 on Christmas morning. A straightforward *Book of Common Prayer* Holy Communion, this service is quiet and simple, an island of peace and reflection in the midst of a hectic calendar of services, events and family celebrations. Nor have I been alone in my preference, for I have always been joined by a sizable group of people. For some, this service is part of their regular spiritual practice and they gather every week, or as often as they can, to share in the solemn and beautiful words of the 17th-century liturgy. Others appreciate it most on the busiest days, when they would not otherwise have an opportunity to pause and give thanks for this most wonderful of gifts. Quiet and unobtrusive, containing only the essentials for prayer and worship, the words slip by, giving space and time to ponder those things that are outside both space and time.

And so, in Matthew's gospel, does the birth of Christ happen. Quietly and unobtrusively, the Saviour of the world is born. His arrival has already caused turmoil to Joseph, and the days after his birth will be eventful and frightening, but just for now there is a gap between events, and it is in this gap, this intake of breath before the next adventure, that the greatest of adventures begins.

A blessed and joyous Christmas to you! Try to find space today to meet God. He will be found, of course, in the midst of the festivities, but he will enter your hearts in the silence in between. If you are spending this day by yourself, allow the silence to take hold and listen for the words of enduring love beyond that silence.

SALLY WELCH

Thursday 26 December — **Matthew 2:1–2, 7–8 (NRSV)**

Wise men?

In the time of King Herod, after Jesus was born in Bethlehem of Judea, wise men from the East came to Jerusalem, asking, 'Where is the child who has been born king of the Jews? For we observed his star at its rising, and have come to pay him homage'... Then Herod secretly called for the wise men and learned from them the exact time when the star had appeared. Then he sent them to Bethlehem, saying, 'Go and search diligently for the child; and when you have found him, bring me word so that I may also go and pay him homage.'

You've got to love those wise men! Travelling a great distance on the inspiration of a star, guided by a knowledge of astronomy and a powerful curiosity, they stroll into Jerusalem, the capital city of an occupied territory, and calmly ask where the new king of the subjugated people may be found. Did they not pause and reflect on the impact this question might have, not only on the Jewish people but on their oppressors, the Romans? Or were they so eager to see this great wonder that they forgot practicalities in their excitement?

And how do such straight-thinking men stand up against the evil genius of Herod, who no doubt learns of their arrival from the network of spies that he would have had in the city and summons them 'secretly' (v. 7), to woo them with praise for their intelligence and diligence and send them off also to spy for him. From the first days after Jesus' birth, his enemies are already gathering, using good people for wrong purposes, tempting and flattering them so that they are swept unwittingly into the net of lies and deceit that is being woven against the Saviour of the world.

But in Christ, the redemption of the world has already been achieved, because the incarnation lies beyond the boundaries of time and space. No evil can stand against the power of good, however desperate the situation might seem. No good is ever wasted, however slight it might appear in the face of cruelty and wickedness.

Lord Jesus, thank you for your gifts of hope and love,
of light in the darkness and joy in the morning.

SALLY WELCH

Friday 27 December — Matthew 2:9–11 (NRSV)

Journey's end – or beginning?

When they had heard the king, they set out; and there, ahead of them, went the star that they had seen at its rising, until it stopped over the place where the child was. When they saw that the star had stopped, they were overwhelmed with joy. On entering the house, they saw the child with Mary his mother; and they knelt down and paid him homage. Then, opening their treasure-chests, they offered him gifts of gold, frankincense, and myrrh.

With their arrival in Jerusalem, the wise men have set off a chain of consequences that will lead to the mass slaughter of infants and the narrow escape from death and flight into exile of the very child they sought. But for the moment all that is in the future.

Here, we see the culmination of months of gazing out at the dark star-scattered sky, trying to work out the movement of stars and planets and what they might mean. Here, we see the result of the difficult decision to put everyday life on hold for an indefinite time and set out on a lengthy, perilous journey on no greater evidence than a new star and a hope for its meaning. Here, hard work and effort are finally repaid and the wise men, 'overwhelmed with joy' (v. 10), sink to their knees, acknowledging the arrival of a king whose greatness perhaps even they don't fully understand. The symbolic gifts are offered: gold for kingship, frankincense for priesthood and myrrh for death and sorrow. Even in the midst of rejoicing, the first hints of what is to come are present.

And what does the arrival of the wise men mean for us? A validation of our faith as something not just for the susceptible or vulnerable? A sign that following Christ is for all people, rich and poor, wise and unschooled? Yes, these things, but perhaps also a reminder from history to celebrate the good times, to mark the occasions when things turn out right, when our preparations and effort bring just rewards and to savour our moments of triumph, however small.

Lord, help me to make the most of my successes, to rejoice in times of good fortune and to share my delight with generosity to others.

SALLY WELCH

Saturday 28 December   **Matthew 2:12, 16 (NRSV)**

Who is to blame?

And having been warned in a dream not to return to Herod, they left for their own country by another road... When Herod saw that he had been tricked by the wise men, he was infuriated, and he sent and killed all the children in and around Bethlehem who were two years old or under, according to the time that he had learned from the wise men.

And so the all-too-brief interlude draws to a close. The wise men have studied hard, travelled far, searched diligently and been rewarded with the opportunity of presenting their gifts to the Messiah. The baby king has, in his turn, given them the gift of satisfaction in a goal well met and a life-changing encounter. In history, the work of the wise men is completed, although they still have to return to the lands they came from.

But not even the first step of the long journey home is without its challenges, for they are 'warned in a dream not to return to Herod' (v. 12). Sensitive to the wisdom that can be found in the passage of the stars and the whispering of dreams, they obey this mystical instruction and set off on a new and unfamiliar route homewards. Their part in this story has ended; it is those who are left who face the appalling retaliation of Herod, who, in his anger at being tricked and his fear of being usurped by a new Jewish king and his followers, sends out the horrific edict that results in the massacre of all Jewish infants in the area.

What might those eastern sages have felt if they had known the consequences of their actions? What feelings of horror and guilt would have stricken them? The responsibility for the deed does not rest with them, however, but with Herod, who chose this savage course of action, born of his greed for power and his fear that it might be taken from him. He alone must take the blame as the cries of infants and parents chase him through history.

'Hear my prayer, Lord; listen to my cry for mercy' (Psalm 86:6, NIV).

SALLY WELCH

Sunday 29 December — Matthew 2:17–18 (NRSV)

Rachel weeps

Then was fulfilled what had been spoken through the prophet Jeremiah: 'A voice was heard in Ramah, wailing and loud lamentation, Rachel weeping for her children; she refused to be consoled, because they are no more.'

The record of Herod's actions against the infants of Bethlehem blights the atmosphere of joy and hope for the future of the world that Matthew has created in his narration of the quiet peace of Jesus' arrival. It seems as if things have taken a step backwards, to the dark times of Jeremiah, when Jerusalem was captured and the children of Israel taken prisoner and removed to exile in Babylon. It is at Ramah that they were reminded that this exile was the direct consequence of their actions: 'all of you sinned against the Lord and did not obey his voice. Therefore this thing has come upon you' (Jeremiah 40:3). The picture of Rachel mourning for her children has become a symbol not only of all mothers weeping for their lost children, but also of the sorrow of God for his own people.

But there is still hope, even in the darkest of times: Jeremiah promises the desperate exiles that: 'there is hope for your future… your children shall come back to their own country' (Jeremiah 31:17). Legend has it that Rachel's tomb is in Bethlehem, so Matthew links the darkness and despair of the past with the hope of redemption for all time – past, present and future – which is held in Jesus. We are reminded once more that sorrow and joy are part of the human condition. The dark and the light threads are twisted together for now, inextricably entwined. But this will not always be so; there will be rejoicing in Jerusalem, and Rachel will cease to weep when she is reunited once more with those she loves.

Lord Jesus, let us not be afraid to mourn those whom we have lost, but grant us also the grace to wait patiently for the time of fulfilment, when God will turn our mourning into joy, will comfort us and give us gladness for sorrow: 'their life shall become like a watered garden, and they shall never languish again' (Jeremiah 31:12).

SALLY WELCH

Monday 30 December   **Matthew 2:13–15a (NRSV)**

Keeping faith alive

Now after they had left, an angel of the Lord appeared to Joseph in a dream and said, 'Get up, take the child and his mother, and flee to Egypt, and remain there until I tell you; for Herod is about to search for the child, to destroy him.' Then Joseph got up, took the child and his mother by night, and went to Egypt, and remained there until the death of Herod.

And what of Jesus and his parents during these times of darkness and terror? His life, too, is not without its challenges. Once again, an angel appears to Joseph in a dream and gives him instructions.

By what exercise of faith does Joseph act upon this dream! How hard it must have been to gather up his son and his wife and travel the desperate miles into exile in Egypt. How great the temptation must have been to disregard the words of the angel as something born of excitement or imagination, fevered by the visit of the wise men and the magnificence of their gifts. What courage and energy must have gone into the difficult journey and the subsequent years of living in Egypt. A carpenter's skills must be in demand everywhere, but life cannot have been easy for the refugees, forced by unexpected events out of the regular pattern of their everyday lives. How they must have longed for their homeland, and wondered if they would ever see their native town again. Only their great faith in God would have sustained them, keeping hope alive and trusting that when the time was right they would be able to return to their home and families.

So too for us, when our life's road is full of unexpected twists and turns, when all that we had counted as certainty vanishes and the predictable pattern of days is disrupted. Then we must wait patiently upon the Lord, trusting in his good purposes for us, never losing hope and working to make the best of the circumstances in which we find ourselves, however strange they may be.

Lord, turn our eyes towards our eternal home,
knowing that there, at least, will we find rest and peace.

SALLY WELCH

Tuesday 31 December   **Matthew 2:19–23 (NRSV, abridged)**

Jesus of Nazareth

When Herod died, an angel of the Lord suddenly appeared in a dream to Joseph in Egypt and said, 'Get up, take the child and his mother, and go to the land of Israel, for those who were seeking the child's life are dead.' Then Joseph got up, took the child and his mother, and went to the land of Israel… And after being warned in a dream, he went away to the district of Galilee. There he made his home in a town called Nazareth, so that what had been spoken through the prophets might be fulfilled, 'He will be called a Nazorean.'

And so the story of Jesus' birth as told by Matthew comes to an end. It is a strange tale, one full of dreams and prophecies, where angels give warnings and advice. The arrival of Jesus himself is told in one short sentence, and we are told nothing about the circumstances of his birth. Mary herself plays a tiny part, seemingly simply the human vehicle for the divine event, a far cry from the active participant in the world's redemption described in Luke's version. The action is with the men, with Joseph and the visitors from the east, whose ears are attuned to the realm of God and whose faith is strong enough to act upon stars and dreams. We are not spared the darker side of the story, and the cries of infants and mothers in pain echo down the centuries, tearing at our hearts.

But in all this God's plan prevails. From the first days the means whereby the redemption of God's children will be fulfilled are assured. The prophets sing to us of a Messiah; the generations build one upon another, son after son, from Abraham to David and thence to Jesus, son of Joseph the carpenter, 'called a Nazorean' (v. 23).

The faithful listen to the words of God and act upon them with courage and faith. The wicked are defeated, and God's will is done on earth.

'And a voice from heaven said, "This is my son, the Beloved, with whom I am well pleased"' (Matthew 3:17).

SALLY WELCH

This page is left blank for your notes

Overleaf… Reading *New Daylight* in a group | Author profile | Recommended reading | Order and subscription forms

Reading *New Daylight* in a group

SALLY WELCH

I am aware that although some of you cherish the moments of quiet during the day that enable you to read and reflect on the passages we offer you in *New Daylight*, other readers prefer to study in small groups, to enable conversation and discussion and the sharing of insights. With this in mind, here are some ideas for discussion starters within a study group. Some of the questions are generic and can be applied to any set of contributions within this issue; others are specific to certain sets of readings. I hope they generate some interesting reflections and conversations!

General discussion starters

These can be used for any study series within this issue. Remember there are no right or wrong answers – these questions are simply to enable a group to engage in conversation.

- What do you think the main idea or theme of the author in this series? Do you think they succeeded in communicating this to you, or were you more interested in the side issues?
- Have you had any experience of the issues that are raised in the study? How have they affected your life?
- What evidence does the author use to support their ideas? Do they use personal observations and experience, facts, quotations from other authorities? Which appeals to you most?
- Does the author make a 'call to action'? Is that call realistic and achievable? Do you think their ideas will work in the secular world?
- Can you identify specific passages that struck you personally – as interesting, profound, difficult to understand or illuminating?
- Did you learn something new reading this series? Will you think differently about some things, and if so, what are they?

Questions for specific series

Success and failure (Veronica Zundel)

'Apparent success is really failure and apparent failure really success.' How far do you agree with this statement as it is demonstrated in the Bible? Do you agree with it in reference to your own life? Do you learn more from your failures than your successes?

Francis and Clare (Helen Julian CSF)

Francis experienced a personal conflict between his desire to share his faith with others and his need to withdraw into contemplative prayer. How do we find a balance between prayer and action in our own lives? Have our church communities got it right or is one element over-emphasised? If so, how might this be corrected?

Christmas in Matthew (Sally Welch)

The first 16 verses of Matthew's gospel describe the genealogy of Jesus. How have your parents influenced your faith journey? What other teachers have there been along the way? What ways can we use to share the story of Jesus with the next generation?

Psalm 119 (Stephen Rand)

Which passages in the Bible have helped you understand the nature of God? Are there prayers or passages from scripture that you have learnt by heart because they mean so much to you? Is there a way in which you could share these with others?

'Your word is a lamp to my feet and a light to my path' (Psalm 119:105, NRSV).

Author profile: Geoffrey Lowson

You spent 21 years working for USPG. What sort of work did you do there?

I joined USPG in 1984 as what was then known as an area secretary, representing the society in various dioceses in the north. The work was multifaceted, but involved preaching, speaking engagements and work in schools. I counted once that I had preached in about 700 churches over those years. The brief was to teach about mission in its broadest sense whenever and however the opportunity arose. At that time, USPG had a substantial programme providing the opportunity for overseas clergy and others to study or gain experience in this country – I was involved in finding placements for them. I particularly enjoyed that.

You have also been a parish priest. Which aspects of this appealed to you most – and least?

To be honest, I enjoyed it all, but I loved preparing and leading worship and preaching. And visiting; I guess that in terms of modern practice I was rather old-fashioned in that I did a lot of pastoral visiting. Least liked? If I was really pushed to answer, deanery synod meetings. Apologies to any area deans!

What parts of being a Christian do you struggle with?

One of my hobby horses is that the church should have what I describe as 'fuzzy edges'. In other words, in the parish there should be a blurred border between the 'church community' and the wider community. I find it difficult when people want a narrow and exclusive church.

How has your prayer life changed or developed over the years?

Confession time! While I have, of course, said my prayers, I have never been too good in terms of a structured prayer life. However, I can say with hand on heart that I have been disciplined when it came to sermon preparation and preparing worship. I think that in a way my prayer life was somehow embedded in that.

Now that you have retired, are you busier than ever?

I have always enjoyed being busy and so perhaps 'busier than ever' is not quite the right phrase, but I am certainly very busy and happily so. There is so much to do in the years that are left.

Recommended reading

What can we learn from Augustine? There are many books that tell the life story of Augustine and how he has been fundamental in shaping western Christian theology and practice. This is not one of them. This book is about how he became a Christian – the problems he faced; the doubts he struggled with. It is about how he made sense of his belief in God, and shared it with other people. It is about how he learned to read the Bible and to pray. And it is about the word that is at the heart of his Christian life – love. It concludes with moments of prayer from Augustine's life, in which he glimpses visions of God, encouraging the reader to take their own next steps in discipleship.

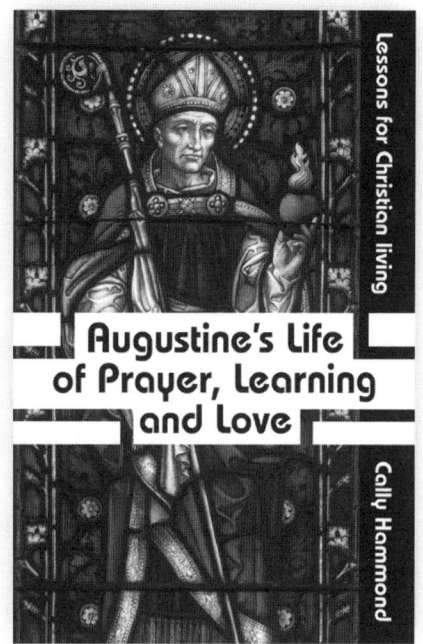

This is an edited excerpt from Chapter 2, 'Augustine's journey towards faith'.

On one level every human story is the same: we are born, we live and we die. On another level, every human story is different: we are born into wealth or poverty, peace or war, nurture or exploitation, education or ignorance, conformism or rebellion. Our identities are made up of a mixture of factors – genes, parental influence, peer pressure, public goals and private dreams.

Augustine's story is no different. He belongs in history, his own time, as we do in ours. But he also belongs to all time, because for 1,600 years people have been meeting him through his writings, listening to him and finding him to be a reliable guide for Christian discipleship. No one could be more aware than he was that life is limited and that our human vision and understanding are partial and imperfect. But he was also convinced that for faithful Christians the story of one life can be the story of every life. And so, in his early years as an adult Christian, he sits down to write his *Confessions*. What we find out about him in this chapter comes from that book. It is so small compared to some of his other works, but so massive in terms of its influence and power, and the effect it has on almost everyone who reads it.

We can't look at the whole story in detail, so instead I have selected for us to explore together some key moments in Augustine's life up to the time of his conversion. These are moments that show us universal human experiences and give voice to universal questions: what is sin really about? Why do so many people live their life in fear? How is it that our dreams and our reality fail to match up to each other? What does it mean to become a Christian, to repent and to be baptised? They are all only moments, only fragments of a life, but they are moments common to many of us. That will help us to get to grips with the power of Augustine's faith and with his potential to inspire faith in us and in others. This is essential before we turn to the difficult questions of ideas and beliefs about God (what some Christians call 'theology'). Understanding the man will give us the confidence to learn from him and to tackle new ways of praying that perhaps always seemed way beyond us. It could be a rollercoaster ride!

Augustine was very clever. He knew it, too. But being so clever did not make him happy. Instead he could not understand why his being intelligent didn't help him live his life better. He used his cleverness to win praise from people, instead of seeking God's approval. But he knew their praise was worthless, even though he was desperate to win such admiration. In reality, he knew that they were only judging him according to what they saw on the surface, not according to the deep-down reality of his confused, disordered self. He couldn't help notice how often people condemned trivial faults in others, but didn't worry about their own serious character flaws or abusive behaviour. Being a fundamentally honest person, Augustine knew he too was guilty of such hypocrisy:

> *In schoolboy games I was desperate to excel, and strove to win, even if it meant cheating. I was determined not to let others cheat me, and denounced them harshly if I spotted it, but I was doing the exact same thing to them! If I was caught in the act, I chose to get angry rather than to admit the truth. So much for the innocence of youth. There is no such thing, Lord!*

It is hard to read that and not think of cheating scandals in sport, like the case of cyclist Lance Armstrong. Such attitudes are constant down the years. So is the Christian challenge to them – a challenge to be honest, whatever the cost; a challenge to put truth before personal vanity. There is also the Christian belief, rooted in the apostle Paul's equally hard-won life experience, that sometimes to lose is to win.

> *Human failings are the same from the childhood time of carers and teachers, trivia and playtimes, as in the adult transition to citizenship, work, and money – they are exactly the same! But more severe punishments take the place of discipline fit for children.*

Some people think that Christianity is obsessed with sin. That is not true, but sin is a vital part of understanding our relationship with God. Unless we are honest about our failings we cannot make any progress in that relationship. Augustine was firmly convinced that we are responsible for our own failings. We cannot shuffle off responsibility by blaming them on upbringing or circumstances. Somehow, we have to accept that they are part of who we are. Only then can we move forward and begin to live life with the freedom of the gospel.

Admitting our sinfulness is liberating! Once we have confessed the worst, we can get to work on becoming who God would have us be. This is the process Augustine shows us in his *Confessions*. In one way, it is like a long riff on Paul's experience in the New Testament – a move away from the kind of faith that is all about judgement and repression to a faith which is 'the glorious liberty of the children of God'.

To order a copy of this book, please use the order form on page 149.

AVAILABLE NOW: **NEW HOLY HABITS** RESOURCES

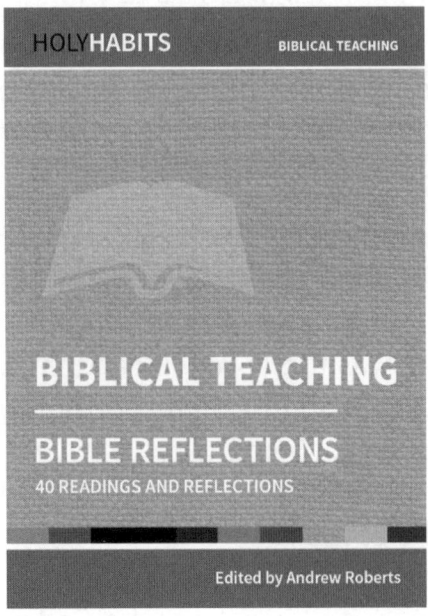

   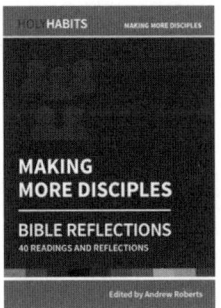

Holy Habits is an all-age initiative to nurture and develop Christian discipleship. It explores Luke's model of church found in Acts 2:42–47, identifies ten habits and encourages the development of a way of life formed by them.

These new additions to the Holy Habits resources have been developed to help churches and individuals explore the Holy Habits through prayerful engagement with the Bible and live them out in whole-life, missional discipleship.

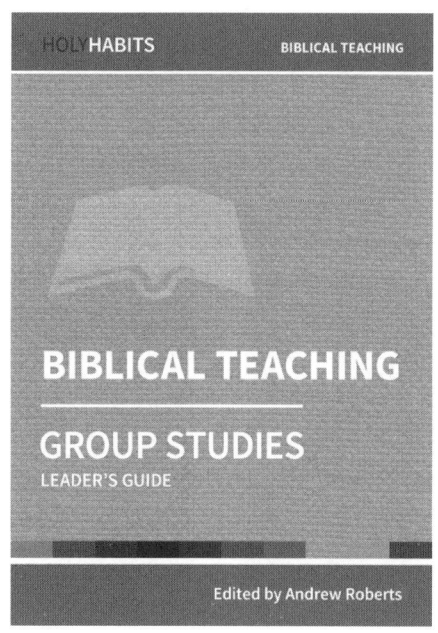

Holy Habits Bible Reflections
Edited by Andrew Roberts
£4.99

Holy Habits Group Studies
Edited by Andrew Roberts
£6.99

Available March 2020:
SERVING | SHARING RESOURCES | GLADNESS AND GENEROSITY | WORSHIP | BREAKING BREAD

Find out more at brfonline.org.uk/holy-habits

Really Useful Guides

  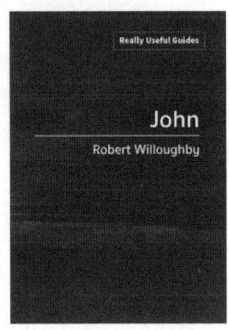 

Each Really Useful Guide focuses on a specific biblical book, making it come to life for the reader, enabling them to understand the message and to apply its truth to today's circumstances. Though not a commentary, it gives valuable insight into the book's message. Though not an introduction, it summarises the important aspects of the book to aid reading and application.

Genesis 1—11
Rebecca Watson
978 0 85746 791 1 £6.99

John
Robert Willoughby
978 0 85746 751 5 £6.99

Psalms
Simon P. Stock
978 0 85746 731 7 £6.99

Colossians and Philemon
Derek Tidball
978 0 85746 730 0 £5.99

brfonline.org.uk

To order

Online: **brfonline.org.uk**
Telephone: +44 (0)1865 319700
Mon–Fri 9.15–17.30

Delivery times within the UK are normally 15 working days. Prices are correct at the time of going to press but may change without prior notice.

Title	Price	Qty	Total
Augustine's Life of Prayer, Learning and Love	£9.99		
Really Useful Guides: Genesis 1—11	£6.99		
Really Useful Guides: Psalms	£6.99		
Really Useful Guides: John	£6.99		
Really Useful Guides: Colossians and Philemon	£5.99		

POSTAGE AND PACKING CHARGES			
Order value	UK	Europe	Rest of world
Under £7.00	£2.00	£5.00	£7.00
£7.00–£29.99	£3.00	£9.00	£15.00
£30.00 and over	FREE	£9.00 + 15% of order value	£15.00 + 20% of order value

Total value of books	
Postage and packing	
Total for this order	

Please complete in BLOCK CAPITALS

Title _____ First name/initials _____ Surname _____

Address _____

_____ Postcode _____

Acc. No. _____ Telephone _____

Email _____

Method of payment

☐ Cheque (made payable to BRF)   ☐ MasterCard / Visa

Card no. ☐☐☐☐ ☐☐☐☐ ☐☐☐☐ ☐☐☐☐

Expires end M M Y Y   Security code* ☐☐☐   Last 3 digits on the reverse of the card

Signature* _____ Date _____ / _____ / _____

*ESSENTIAL IN ORDER TO PROCESS YOUR ORDER

Please return this form to:
BRF, 15 The Chambers, Vineyard, Abingdon OX14 3FE | **enquiries@brf.org.uk**
To read our terms and find out about cancelling your order, please visit **brfonline.org.uk/terms**.

The Bible Reading Fellowship (BRF) is a Registered Charity (233280)

How to encourage Bible reading in your church

BRF has been helping individuals connect with the Bible for over 90 years. We want to support churches as they seek to encourage church members into regular Bible reading.

Order a Bible reading resources pack

This pack is designed to give your church the tools to publicise our Bible reading notes. It includes:

- Sample Bible reading notes for your congregation to try.
- Publicity resources, including a poster.
- A church magazine feature about Bible reading notes.

The pack is free, but we welcome a £5 donation to cover the cost of postage. If you require a pack to be sent outside the UK or require a specific number of sample Bible reading notes, please contact us for postage costs. More information about what the current pack contains is available on our website.

How to order and find out more

- Visit **biblereadingnotes.org.uk/for-churches**
- Telephone BRF on +44 (0)1865 319700 Mon–Fri 9.15–17.30
- Write to us at BRF, 15 The Chambers, Vineyard, Abingdon OX14 3FE

Keep informed about our latest initiatives

We are continuing to develop resources to help churches encourage people into regular Bible reading, wherever they are on their journey. Join our email list at **brfonline.org.uk/signup** to stay informed about the latest initiatives that your church could benefit from.

Transforming lives and communities

BRF is a charity that is passionate about making a difference through the Christian faith. We want to see lives and communities transformed through our creative programmes and resources for individuals, churches and schools. We are doing this by resourcing:

- **Christian growth and understanding of the Bible.** Through our Bible reading notes, books, digital resources, conferences and other events, we're resourcing individuals, groups and leaders in churches for their own spiritual journey and for their ministry.
- **Church outreach in the local community.** BRF is the home of Messy Church and The Gift of Years, programmes that churches are embracing to great effect as they seek to engage with their communities.
- **Teaching Christianity in primary schools.** Our Barnabas in Schools team is working with primary-aged children and their teachers, enabling them to explore Christianity creatively and confidently within the school curriculum.
- **Children's and family ministry.** Through our Parenting for Faith programme, websites and published resources, we're working with churches and families, enabling children and adults alike to explore Christianity creatively and bring the Bible alive.

Do you share our vision?

Sales of our books and Bible reading notes cover the cost of producing them. However, our other programmes are funded primarily by donations, grants and legacies. If you share our vision, would you help us to transform even more lives and communities? Your prayers and financial support are vital for the work that we do. You could:

- support BRF's ministry with a regular donation (at **brf.org.uk/donate**);
- support us with a one-off gift (use the form on pages 153–54);
- consider leaving a gift to BRF in your will (see page 152);
- encourage your church to support BRF as part of your church's giving to home mission – perhaps focusing on a specific area of our ministry, or a particular member of our Barnabas in Schools team.
- most important of all, support BRF with your prayers.

Let's build a better world

Today's children are global citizens. Modern technology means that the latest news from across the world can be broadcast in seconds, and communications with North or South America, Africa, Asia or Australasia are simply a click away.

As travel between countries becomes faster, we also tend to move around more. Many of today's children will live alongside people from other countries with different cultures, customs and beliefs. Even within Christianity itself, there can be differences in how the faith is celebrated from one country to the next.

Our Barnabas in Schools team has been exploring this theme all year with schools across England and Wales. Through 'Christianity around the World', they've taken children on a journey to learn about how faith is practised in countries such as Ethiopia, Argentina, Spain and Russia. It's all part of our aim to help the next generation grow to love and accept each other and ultimately build a better world.

How can you help? You can be part of this vision too by leaving a gift in your will to BRF. Gifts in wills help us teach Christianity creatively within the school curriculum, and every year over 20,000 children experience our Barnabas RE Days exploring 'Christianity around the World' and other themes.

Gifts in wills don't need to be huge to help us make a real difference and, for every £1 we receive, we typically invest 95p back into charitable activities.

For further information about making a gift to BRF in your will, please visit **brf.org.uk/lastingdifference**, contact us at **+44 (0)1865 319700** or email **giving@brf.org.uk**.

Whatever you can do or give, we thank you for your support.

> Pray. Give. Get involved.
> **brf.org.uk**

SHARING OUR VISION – MAKING A GIFT

I would like to make a gift to support BRF. Please use my gift for:

☐ where it is needed most ☐ Barnabas in Schools ☐ Parenting for Faith
☐ Messy Church ☐ The Gift of Years

| Title | First name/initials | Surname |

| Address |

| | Postcode |

| Email |

| Telephone |

| Signature | Date |

gift aid it You can add an extra 25p to every £1 you give.

Please treat as Gift Aid donations all qualifying gifts of money made

☐ today, ☐ in the past four years, ☐ and in the future.

I am a UK taxpayer and understand that if I pay less Income Tax and/or Capital Gains Tax in the current tax year than the amount of Gift Aid claimed on all my donations, it is my responsibility to pay any difference.

☐ My donation does not qualify for Gift Aid.

Please notify BRF if you want to cancel this Gift Aid declaration, change your name or home address, or no longer pay sufficient tax on your income and/or capital gains.

Please complete other side of form ➡

Please return this form to:
BRF, 15 The Chambers, Vineyard, Abingdon OX14 3FE

The Bible Reading Fellowship is a Registered Charity (233280)

SHARING OUR VISION – MAKING A GIFT

Regular giving

By Direct Debit: You can set up a Direct Debit quickly and easily at **brf.org.uk/donate**

By Standing Order: Please contact our Fundraising Administrator +44 (0)1865 319700 | **giving@brf.org.uk**

One-off donation

Please accept my gift of:

☐ £10 ☐ £50 ☐ £100 Other £ ☐

by (*delete as appropriate*):

☐ Cheque/Charity Voucher payable to 'BRF'

☐ MasterCard/Visa/Debit card/Charity card

Name on card

Card no.

Expires end M M Y Y Security code*

*Last 3 digits on the reverse of the card
ESSENTIAL IN ORDER TO PROCESS YOUR PAYMENT

Signature

Date

☐ I would like to leave a gift in my will to BRF.

For more information, visit **brf.org.uk/lastingdifference**

For help or advice regarding making a gift, please contact our Fundraising Administrator +44 (0)1865 319700

⬅ Please complete other side of form

Please return this form to:
BRF, 15 The Chambers, Vineyard, Abingdon OX14 3FE

The Bible Reading Fellowship is a Registered Charity (233280)

NEW DAYLIGHT SUBSCRIPTION RATES

Please note our new subscription rates, current until 30 April 2020:

Individual subscriptions
covering 3 issues for under 5 copies, payable in advance (including postage & packing):

	UK	Europe	Rest of world
New Daylight	£17.40	£25.50	£29.40
New Daylight 3-year subscription (9 issues) (not available for Deluxe)	£49.50	N/A	N/A
New Daylight Deluxe per set of 3 issues p.a.	£21.90	£32.40	£38.40

Group subscriptions
covering 3 issues for 5 copies or more, sent to one UK address (post free):

New Daylight	£13.80 per set of 3 issues p.a.
New Daylight Deluxe	£17.55 per set of 3 issues p.a.

Please note that the annual billing period for group subscriptions runs from 1 May to 30 April.

Overseas group subscription rates
Available on request. Please email **enquiries@brf.org.uk**.

Copies may also be obtained from Christian bookshops:

New Daylight	£4.60 per copy
New Daylight Deluxe	£5.85 per copy

All our Bible reading notes can be ordered online by visiting **biblereadingnotes.org.uk/subscriptions**

New Daylight is also available as an app for Android, iPhone and iPad
biblereadingnotes.org.uk/apps

NEW DAYLIGHT INDIVIDUAL SUBSCRIPTION FORM

All our Bible reading notes can be ordered online by visiting **biblereadingnotes.org.uk/subscriptions**

☐ I would like to take out a subscription:

Title _____ First name/initials _____ Surname _____

Address _____

_____ Postcode _____

Telephone _____ Email _____

Please send *New Daylight* beginning with the January 2020 / May 2020 / September 2020 issue (*delete as appropriate*):

(*please tick box*)	UK	Europe	Rest of world
New Daylight 1-year subscription	☐ £17.40	☐ £25.50	☐ £29.40
New Daylight 3-year subscription	☐ £49.50	N/A	N/A
New Daylight Deluxe	☐ £21.90	☐ £32.40	☐ £38.40

Total enclosed £ _____ (cheques should be made payable to 'BRF')

Please charge my MasterCard / Visa ☐ Debit card ☐ with £ _____

Card no. ☐☐☐☐ ☐☐☐☐ ☐☐☐☐ ☐☐☐☐

Expires end ☐☐ / ☐☐ Security code* ☐☐☐ Last 3 digits on the reverse of the card

Signature* _____ Date _____ / _____ / _____

*ESSENTIAL IN ORDER TO PROCESS YOUR PAYMENT

To set up a Direct Debit, please also complete the Direct Debit instruction on page 159 and return it to BRF with this form.

Please return this form with the appropriate payment to:
BRF, 15 The Chambers, Vineyard, Abingdon OX14 3FE

To read our terms and find out about cancelling your order, please visit **brfonline.org.uk/terms**.

The Bible Reading Fellowship is a Registered Charity (233280)

NEW DAYLIGHT GIFT SUBSCRIPTION FORM

☐ I would like to give a gift subscription (please provide both names and addresses):

Title _____ First name/initials _____ Surname _____

Address _____

_____ Postcode _____

Telephone _____ Email _____

Gift subscription name _____

Gift subscription address _____

_____ Postcode _____

Gift message (20 words max. or include your own gift card):

_____

_____

Please send *New Daylight* beginning with the January 2020 / May 2020 / September 2020 issue (*delete as appropriate*):

(*please tick box*)	UK	Europe	Rest of world
New Daylight 1-year subscription	☐ £17.40	☐ £25.50	☐ £29.40
New Daylight 3-year subscription	☐ £49.50	N/A	N/A
New Daylight Deluxe	☐ £21.90	☐ £32.40	☐ £38.40

Total enclosed £ _____ (cheques should be made payable to 'BRF')

Please charge my MasterCard / Visa ☐ Debit card ☐ with £ _____

Card no. ☐☐☐☐ ☐☐☐☐ ☐☐☐☐ ☐☐☐☐

Expires end ☐☐☐☐   Security code* ☐☐☐   Last 3 digits on the reverse of the card

Signature* _____ Date _____ /_____ /_____

*ESSENTIAL IN ORDER TO PROCESS YOUR PAYMENT

To set up a Direct Debit, please also complete the Direct Debit instruction on page 159 and return it to BRF with this form.

Please return this form with the appropriate payment to:
BRF, 15 The Chambers, Vineyard, Abingdon OX14 3FE

To read our terms and find out about cancelling your order, please visit **brfonline.org.uk/terms**.

The Bible Reading Fellowship is a Registered Charity (233280)

DIRECT DEBIT PAYMENT

You can pay for your annual subscription to our Bible reading notes using Direct Debit. You need only give your bank details once, and the payment is made automatically every year until you cancel it. If you would like to pay by Direct Debit, please use the form opposite, entering your BRF account number under 'Reference number'.

You are fully covered by the Direct Debit Guarantee:

The Direct Debit Guarantee

- This Guarantee is offered by all banks and building societies that accept instructions to pay Direct Debits.
- If there are any changes to the amount, date or frequency of your Direct Debit, The Bible Reading Fellowship will notify you 10 working days in advance of your account being debited or as otherwise agreed. If you request The Bible Reading Fellowship to collect a payment, confirmation of the amount and date will be given to you at the time of the request.
- If an error is made in the payment of your Direct Debit, by The Bible Reading Fellowship or your bank or building society, you are entitled to a full and immediate refund of the amount paid from your bank or building society.
- If you receive a refund you are not entitled to, you must pay it back when The Bible Reading Fellowship asks you to.
- You can cancel a Direct Debit at any time by simply contacting your bank or building society. Written confirmation may be required. Please also notify us.

The Bible Reading Fellowship

Instruction to your bank or building society to pay by Direct Debit

Please fill in the whole form using a ballpoint pen and return it to:
BRF, 15 The Chambers, Vineyard, Abingdon OX14 3FE

Service User Number: | 5 | 5 | 8 | 2 | 2 | 9 |

Name and full postal address of your bank or building society

To: The Manager	Bank/Building Society
Address	
	Postcode

Name(s) of account holder(s)

Branch sort code

Bank/Building Society account number

Reference number

Instruction to your Bank/Building Society
Please pay The Bible Reading Fellowship Direct Debits from the account detailed in this instruction, subject to the safeguards assured by the Direct Debit Guarantee. I understand that this instruction may remain with The Bible Reading Fellowship and, if so, details will be passed electronically to my bank/building society.

Signature(s)

Banks and Building Societies may not accept Direct Debit instructions for some types of account.

ND0319

BRF

Transforming lives and communities

Christian growth and understanding of the Bible

Resourcing individuals, groups and leaders in churches for their own spiritual journey and for their ministry

Church outreach in the local community

Offering two programmes that churches are embracing to great effect as they seek to engage with their local communities and transform lives

Teaching Christianity in primary schools

Working with children and teachers to explore Christianity creatively and confidently

Children's and family ministry

Working with churches and families to explore Christianity creatively and bring the Bible alive

parenting for faith

Visit **brf.org.uk** for more information on BRF's work

brf.org.uk

The Bible Reading Fellowship (BRF) is a Registered Charity (No. 233280)